W9-BAG-002

Cognitive Patterns: Problem-Solving Frameworks for Object Technology

Managing Object Technology Series

Charles F. Bowman
Series Editor
and
President
SoftWright Solutions
Suffern, New York

Additional Volumes in Preparation

Cognitive Patterns: Problem-Solving Frameworks for Object Technology

Karen M. Gardner, Ph.D. • Alexander R. Rush
Michael Crist • Robert Konitzer
Bobbin Teegarden

PUBLISHED BY THE PRESS SYNDICATE OF THE UNIVERSITY OF CAMBRIDGE
The Pitt Building, Trumpington Street, Cambridge CB2 1RP, United Kingdom

CAMBRIDGE UNIVERSITY PRESS
The Edinburgh Building, Cambridge CB2 2RU, UK
http://www.cup.cam.ac.uk
40 West 20th Street, New York, NY 10011-4211, USA
http://www.cup.org
10 Stamford Road, Oakleigh, Melbourne 3166, Australia

Published in association with SIGS Books & Multimedia

© 1998 Cambridge University Press

All rights reserved.

This book is in copyright. Subject to statutory exception and to the provisions of relevant collective licensing agreements, no reproduction of any part may take place without the written permission of Cambridge University Press.

Any product mentioned in this book may be a trademark of its company.

First published in 1998

Design and composition by Kevin Callahan
Cover design by Yin Moy

Printed in the United States of America

A catalog record for this book is available from the British Library

Library of Congress Cataloging-in-Publication Data is available.

ISBN 0-521-64998-6 paperback

To Suzanne, Rachel, and Nina, for their love, patience,
and understanding during many late nights. —AR

To Dawne, Hilary, and Lauren Crist —MC

To June Singer, who really started it all —KG

To Jean, Mimi, Mac, and Drew (age 1) who
"prowled and growled" throughout the entire effort. —BK

To Porter —BT

Contents

About the Authors

Robert Konitzer has worked in information technology since 1986, with a focus on the pragmatics of software development. He has worked extensively on the architecture and design of distributed client/server systems since 1989. He holds an MBA degree with an emphasis in MIS and Operations Research from the University of Denver. (Bob_Konitzer@clrmnt.com)

Alexander Rush has held a variety of positions in information technology since 1983, with an emphasis in knowledge analysis and object-oriented analysis and design. He has been a practitioner of KADS Object for the past six years, with experience in cognitive modeling applied to object-oriented analysis and design, knowledge engineering and management, and enterprise object modeling. (Alex_Rush@clrmnt.com)

Michael K. Crist has worked in information technology since 1983. He has participated in all phases of object-oriented software development, including project management, testing and performance engineering, object modeling, and OO technical and application architecture design. He holds degrees in anthropology and biostatistics. (Michael_Crist@clrmnt.com)

Karen M. Gardner, Ph.D., has worked in information technology since 1977 and with objects for over 10 years. She specializes in object-oriented analysis/design, distributed intelligent objects, cognitive modeling of business processes, knowledge analysis, and project management. She has participated in all phases of the life cycle of object-oriented projects. (Karen_Gardner@clrmnt.com)

Bobbin Teegarden has been a business engineering consultant and IT technology professional longer than she cares to admit. Her current specialization is in enterprise knowledge modeling of complex systems and business application architecture and design using object-oriented and Expert Systems techniques. Her professional background experience has spanned systems engineering to management consulting. She is currently working on applying complexity and chaos theories to business modeling and application architecture. (teegardenb@aol.com)

Foreword

As systems become more complex, the human limitations to comprehending system requirements become more evident. Since we cannot develop appropriate solutions if we do not understand the problem, human understanding is the key ingredient.

Cognitive Patterns addresses this central issue by providing techniques for system specification that are based on our human facility of thinking and reasoning. As such, it does not model system requirements in terms of programming languages and platforms. Instead, it models the way reality is understood by *people*. Furthermore, this "cognitive" approach permits us to analyze *any* area of human reality—not just that of data processing. Using the techniques described in this book, we are no longer restricted to data processing applications. We can develop object-oriented systems that involve the interaction of machines, people, *and* computers.

Cognitive Patterns not only shows us how to develop cognitive-based systems, it provides a comprehensive series of best-practice models and case studies. The book supplies patterns for problem solving, teaches by example, and is based on the firsthand experience of its talented team of authors.

This is an important book for every system developer. It defines how the next generation of systems will be developed.

—James J. Odell

Acknowledgments

We wish to express our sincere thanks to the many individuals who enabled us to complete this book, including our families, friends, and professional colleagues in the object-oriented community.

Susan Blew of Wells Fargo provided a critical review of early drafts of the manuscript. We wish to thank her especially for her consistent support, friendship, and confidence in our work.

Jim Odell has provided the basic premises of our object-oriented thinking and has graciously given many hours of his time in helping us develop the ideas presented in this book.

Jim Trott, a KADS evangelist and practitioner, has provided helpful review and commentary, strange humor, and the case study examples from Boeing included in chapter 5.

Bill Cathcart, an early adapter of KADS techniques applied to knowledge-based and object-oriented systems, has provided ongoing professional guidance, collaboration, and lively political debate.

Don McCubbrey of the University of Denver has provided mentoring and guidance in navigating the evolving and dynamic waters of technical consulting.

There are several clients we would like to acknowledge for their support of our work; we have drawn much of the material in this book from them. They are:

Wells Fargo Bank, Pacific Bell, Bell South, Northrop Corporation, Boeing, Naval Surface Weapons Center, and US West.

Finally, we wish to acknowledge the two other individuals who provided invaluable assistance in completing this book through help in proofreading, editing, graphics, and technical advice: Courtney Broadus and Michael DeCurtis.

PART 1

Introduction to Cognitive Patterns and KADS Object

Summary

Part 1 consists of:
Chapter 1: Introduction to Cognitive Patterns
Chapter 2: Introduction to KADS Object

These chapters will provide the reader with basic knowledge relating to the concepts and terminology of cognitive patterns, the origins and academic background behind theories of cognition, and the value of cognitive patterns as an approach to modeling business systems and processes. In addition, KADS Object will be introduced as a specific approach to cognitive pattern modeling that enables object-oriented views of cognitive patterns. KADS Object will be explained in detail, including specific examples of the deliverables.

Objectives

The objectives of part 1 are:

- To provide the reader with a basic understanding of cognitive patterns and cognitive modeling concepts and terms.

- To explain the uniqueness of cognitive patterns as an approach, and their value in modeling business systems and processes.

- To introduce KADS Object (a non-proprietary set of cognitive patterns) as a specific framework for enabling object-oriented analysis and design.

CHAPTER 1

Introduction to Cognitive Patterns

INTRODUCTION

The term "cognitive" refers to the human facility of thinking and reasoning (Fetzer, 1992; Goldstein and Blackman, 1978; Hashway and Duke, 1992; Langacker, 1987). Our fascination with how we think, reason and solve problems has resulted in over 2000 years' worth of written reflections on these topics. During this century, the study of cognition has focused on several themes, including childhood development (e.g., how do we learn to read and understand what we read?), ways of coping with the limitations of the human mind (e.g., development of computers that can calculate at speeds far exceeding the human brain), and cognitive models (e.g., conceptual models of how we view the world) (ISKO Conference, 1992; Wagman, 1991).

It is the last topic above, cognitive models, and their application to organizational and system processes, that serves as the basis for this book. Examples of simple cognitive models are shown in figure 1.1. A logger's view of a tree is different from an artist's view of the same tree, which is different from a potential Christmas tree purchaser's view.

The term "cognitive pattern" refers to recurring templates that humans use during problem solving/reasoning activities. For instance, a diagnostic pattern guides our efforts when we attempt to discover the cause of a problem. "Design"

FIGURE 1.1. Three Perceptions of a Tree

patterns, as used in the OO community, are generally more detailed and would, in many cases "instantiate" cognitive patterns. This subject is covered later in the following chapters.

It is the premise of this book that the notion of cognitive patterns, applied to organizational and system processes in business, can facilitate a deeper understanding of these processes, and more effective management of the complexity of these processes. It is these benefits that serve as the foundation of the business case for using cognitive patterns as a framework for object-oriented projects.

This book discusses a specific approach to the use of cognitive patterns, KADS Object, that is used very effectively in conjunction with OO (object-oriented) development. Therefore this approach should not be interpreted as "yet another OO analysis and design methodology." Rather, KADS Object offers a unique "cognitive pattern lens" framework from which to view business and system processes. Its use in concert with any OO methodology leads to the creation of robust, understandable and testable OO models and systems.

KADS Object provides one demonstration of a "cognitive pattern" model—a demonstration that is based on a way that humans define and solve problems. Figure 1.2 illustrates the point that applying a KADS Object cognitive "lens" with which to view the four areas covered in this book (OO systems, OO technical architecture, OO business process modeling and OO knowledge-based systems) is but one point of reference. There are other cognitive lenses available, each of

FIGURE 1.2. Different Lens Used to View Objects

which emphasizes a different aspect of the problem/process under examination. For instance, one can study a cognitive model from the point of view of the metaphors which are used to describe it. In addition, there are other noncognitive ways of viewing the four areas mentioned above (e.g., data-flow diagrams), all of which can provide value. However, these views provide a different perspective from the perspective offered by cognitive patterns.

Throughout history, many analytical models and views have been developed that might be labeled "cognitive" only in the sense that humans developed them. However many of these views are not considered cognitive from our perspective because humans do not innately reason nor think in these terms. An example of this kind of view is probability theory. Probability theory has proven very helpful in overcoming some of the limitations of the way people think, but it is not in itself cognitive. Humans do not think in terms of formal probability. Human cognition has its strengths and its weaknesses, and to say that something is cognitive does not necessarily indicate superiority. However, it is the premise of this book that the advantages of human cognition can be used to facilitate our comprehension of the complicated systems (automated and manual) with which we work.

ORGANIZATION OF THIS BOOK

Our goal in writing this book is to introduce the notion of cognitive patterns, providing evidence for its value to object-oriented projects based on our experience. This book should be considered introductory to the subject, and serve as a reference guide. The primary intended audience for this book is OO practitioners who are interested in the modeling and development of OO systems (especially large, complex systems), individuals interested in modeling business processes as collaborating objects, and those interested in knowledge management. The book is organized into three major sections: introductory chapters on cognitive patterns (part one); explanatory chapters relating to our specific approach to cognitive modeling OO systems, KADS Object (part two); and finally chapters relating to best practice applications of KADS Object (part three).

Part one (chapters 1 and 2) introduces the topic of cognition, mental and connectionist models, domains, frameworks, cognitive maps and design patterns. KADS Object is also presented in some detail as a specific approach using cognitive patterns, including the model structures and the process of mapping to objects. The knowledge elicitation techniques helpful in building the KADS Object patterns are covered in chapter three.

Part two (chapters 3–5) examines the specific mappings from the KADS Object model components to OO design elements such as object types, collaborations and behaviors. Also, the diverse areas beyond OO analysis and design to which KADS Object has been applied are explored.

Part three (chapters 6–9) examines cognitive patterns for typical OO development life-cycle activities including testing, technical architecture and reuse. This section concludes with a case-study example, illustrating the interrelationship between these activities, and the benefits of using a cognitive pattern approach throughout the life cycle.

INTRODUCTION TO COGNITION

Mental Models vs. Connectionism

To understand and appreciate the power of cognitive models, and to provide a context for the rest of the book, a brief visit to the sometimes recondite land of cognitive research is required. Although there are varying and hotly contested views of the notion of the mind, the concept of "representation" (i.e., cognitive models) is central to each. Individuals construct internal mental images (i.e., cognitive models) of their thoughts and views of the world in order to make sense of the continual input with which they are assaulted. Figure 1.3 illustrates a kind of internal mental image (a file folder), which an individual might commonly use to categorize a number of facts. Researchers speak of the architecture of the mind, an architecture that contains various cognitive models;

characteristic ways in which individuals conceptually model (i.e., organize, structure and view) their environments. There is evidence that the ability to conceptually model appears to be innate in humans (Anderson, 1983; Fodor,1983; Johnson-Laird,1983; Lakoff. 1987]). However, the interpretation we give to the models appears to be culturally defined (Lakoff, 1987; Lakoff and Johnson, 1980; Lakoff and Turner, 1989). For instance, according to some researchers (Lakoff, 1987), a cognitive model known as the "front/back" orientation is found in all cultures. All humans have an innate capacity to view things as having fronts and backs. However, in western culture our notion of what constitutes, say, the front of a house varies from what another culture may perceive as the front of a house. So the *application* of the "front/back" model varies among cultures, but the underlying *meaning* remains identical.

There are two current competing theories of the mind concerning internal cognitive representations: mental models and connectionism. Mental models were proposed by Johnson-Laird (1983). In it he suggested that individuals innately construct models of the contents of problems, setting up an internal diagram of a situation that is consistent with the given facts of the problem. In other words, a mental representation is created and manipulated to predict and/or

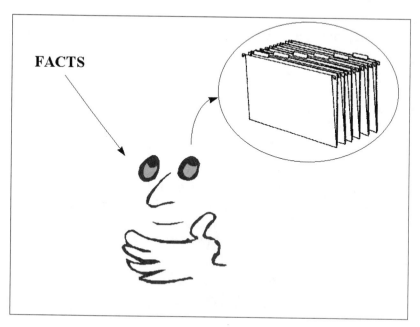

FIGURE 1.3. A Mental Model for Categorizing Facts

cause an outcome. "Tokens" is the term used to represent objects in the world that are manipulated internally. These mental models may be direct analogs to real-world situations/states, as might occur in a simulation model, for example. An opposing opinion is that the internal representation is not necessarily isomorphic to the external world, but is a result of an internal *understanding* of the external world. An artist, for instance, may see a landscape and paint the feelings it evokes rather than painting a realistic portrait of the scene. The idea of mental models was popularized in Senge's book (1990), where the author addresses the set of assumptions (mental models) we bring to any encounter, which then affects the outcome (positive and negative). Meetings held with people who hold different mental models can be stressful as well as stimulating. Figure 1.4 shows various mental models held by individuals during a hypothetical business meeting. One individual views the meeting as a battleground, while others view it as a playground or a sporting event. Inappropriate mental models (such as the "everyone is out to get me" mental model) can cause duress to the individual maintaining that mental model and to the individuals with whom he interacts.

The mental-model approach tends to view the mind as a kind of digital computer, with input, output, storage and processing components, and an emphasis on the internal structure (Block, 1990; Fodor, 1983; Fodor and Pylyshyn, 1988). The competing theory—connectionism (Churchland, 1989; Hinton, 1993)—claims that neural nets (a connection of nodes and links related by associations) provide a more realistic model of how the brain works (and hence how the mind

FIGURE 1.4. Mental Models Used during a Business Meeting

works). Figures 1.4 and 1.5 illustrate the two approaches. Figure 1.4 accentuates the *structure* of the mental models resident within the mind of the participants of the business meeting. Figure 1.5 shows a simplified net which emphasizes the *relationships* between the nodes of a hypothetical connectionist model held by a participant in the same business meeting, also resident within the mind. The role of cognitive models in human problem-solving has been more thoroughly explicated in the mental-model literature than within the connectionist literature. It should also be noted that variations on these two major themes exist in both camps. The specific cognitive patterns addressed in this book possesses characteristics of both, but are presented as examples of mental models.

Several different categories of cognitive patterns/models have been identified (based on both the mental-model approach and the connectionist-model approach), which emphasize one or more of the various aspects of human problem solving, and which are pertinent for this book. Table 1.1 briefly describes the cognitive patterns/models which will be discussed in the remainder of this chapter.

Domains

There is a relatively recent trend within cognitive science to study "domains" (Herschfeld and Gel, 1994). Domain is the name given an innate (or perhaps partially acquired) kind of cognitive pattern used by a perceiving individual that identifies and interprets a class of phenomena assumed to share certain properties (e.g., sorting activities). Implied in this definition is the idea of static and dynamic

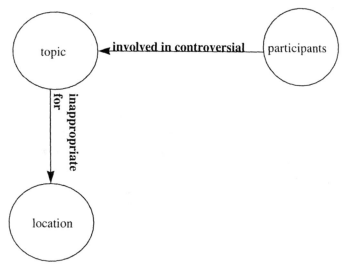

FIGURE 1.5. Business Meeting Mental Models Example

TABLE 1.1. Types of Cognitive Models

Domains	**Goals/principles/reasoning associated with recurring situations; serve as explanatory structure for expectations regarding a situation, as in "sorting activities".**
Frameworks	**Domains with additional context information, as in "sorting mail" activities**
Cognitive Maps	**Frameworks that are oriented towards wayfinding; finding one's way through a problem, as in "sorting mail when address is incomplete".**
Patterns	**Detailed, very context specific instantiations of frameworks, as in "sorting by zipcodes"**

components. For instance, an individual's approach to sorting includes goals, procedures, and a set of core principles that support reasoning about the concepts found in the domain associated with sorting. Every individual uses a variety of these domains. Domains function as a stable response to a set of recurring and complex problems, as in the need to sort items efficiently and effectively. One might envision, then, a set of cognitive patterns called "domains" that are available to individuals that assist them in making sense of the world, especially making sense of recurring situations.

When faced with a situation or problem, we immediately begin to filter and classify the input in order to better manage the information overload created by the influx of data from our situation/problem. Domains are used to partition (i.e., classify) the input by serving as explanatory frames. The structure of domains is not contingent on a particular language, nor is it necessarily accessible to consciousness. The structure of domains appears to be an innate mechanism that reflects the specific relations that exist between the world and our knowledge of it. The content is often culturally dependent. For instance, although the ability to sort appears to be universal, sorting criteria differs widely among different cultures. Figure 1.6 shows an outline of a dwelling as an example of a domain. Although the outline does not show details, the outline does serve as a kind of explanatory frame of expectations regarding our knowledge of dwellings.

Culture, and the specific problem to be solved, defines the content. For example, the domain of grammar (rules that prescribe the use of language) exists in all cultures, but the content of the grammar varies from language to language. Chomsky (1980), however, posited the existence of a universal grammar (an example of a very high-level domain) that would apply to all languages. He based this belief on his clearly articulated notion of domain cognition. If one continues to generalize, one must inevitably discover a generic domain pattern that would apply to all examples of that domain pattern. (However, there is a substantial risk that the generalization can become so vague as to eventually become content free). The most important aspect of domains (from an OO perspective) is that they function as an organized background (i.e., a realm or a context) against which concepts/objects can be identified and classified, and behavior predicted.

Examples of higher-level domains include the aforementioned grammar, designing a tool, or planning a meeting. Examples of lower-level domains include our understanding of notions such as containers, writing utensils, and knives (what they are, how they work, what we can do with them).

Unfortunately the term "domain" has a more narrow definition in computer science, where it refers primarily to the idea of a body of knowledge in some field or subject area, or the set of objects for a given area of interest (e.g., the domain of a billing system, or the domain of operations research, or the domain of telecommunications). By the definition given previously, the field of operations research would incorporate a number of domain patterns. Domain patterns are not specific to a field and thus would exist in other fields as well. For instance, the domain of "sorting" occurs in most, if not all, fields of endeavor.

Frameworks

The notion of a framework has been defined in so many various ways, particularly within the OO community, that it is difficult to present a definition that fits all of the examples of frameworks. From a high level of abstraction, framework patterns have the same general attributes as a "domain" and can probably be viewed as domains with additional context information. Figure 1.7 illustrates the outlines of various kinds of dwellings, showing more specificity than figure 1.6. Figure 1.7 can thus be viewed as a kind of framework when compared with the more generalized figure 1.6.

Frameworks provide a more formal description than would usually apply to a

FIGURE 1.6. Domain Model of a "Dwelling"

FIGURE 1.7. Frameworks for Dwellings

domain. From a systems point of view, frameworks can be considered organizations of situation types that are known to occur commonly during a system life cycle, and which constitute an organizing structure for a system (Mayer et al., 1995) Frameworks have also been described as "medium scale, multipurpose, reusable class hierarchies that depend only on the abstract interfaces of various components and have proven to be valuable tools for simplifying and accelerating further design" (de Champeaux et al., 1993). Firesmith and Eykholt (1995) define frameworks as "any large, reusable, generic specification, design, code, and test pattern of part of an application, consisting primarily of classes (possibly organized into clusters and subframeworks)." At a low level of abstraction, frameworks have been defined as application-specific class libraries that, by

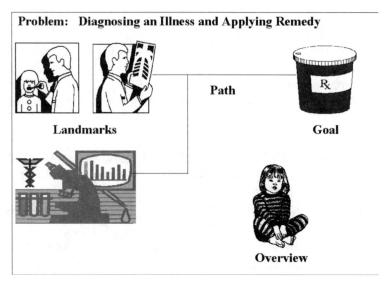

FIGURE 1.8. A Cognitive Map

default, structure the problem solution (Henderson-Sellers, 1992). The most cognitive of the above definitions is Mayer's, which addresses the role of frameworks as providing an organizing structure.

Cognitive maps (Chown et al., 1995) can be considered a specific kind of framework, providing a "mapping" context for applicable domains. Cognitive maps are specialized representations that humans use for "wayfinding." These maps serve two functions. They represent the environment, and they allow a human to move from place to place within mapped environments. While this notion is usually reserved for actual attempts to find one's way in the world, they can be used to describe abstract topics, such as finding one's way through a problem. Figure 1.8 illustrates the notion of a cognitive map for a diagnostic problem. Cognitive maps, as examples of frameworks, consist of four components:

- landmarks (markers for orientation and determining the current location);
- paths (a route to a goal consisting of a sequence of landmarks);
- direction (changing one's relative position in response to a sighting of a landmark or, conversely, because no landmark is visible);
- overviews (provides "bird's-eye views," enabling large-scale reasoning about one's environment).

The term "cognitive map framework" is particularly appropriate for the kind of cognitive pattern to be discussed in the remainder of the book. "KADS Object" is a framework in the sense that it provides a problem-solving/reasoning context (organizing structure) for various domains. For example, the domain of "sorting" is viewed as having a problem-solving/reasoning kind of organizing structure guiding the "sorting" activity. KADS Object is a kind of cognitive map in that it:

1. predicts what landmarks will occur during the problem-solving activity, in terms of the type of objects expected and type of behavior expected at points along the problem-solving way;
2. illustrates a proven directed path to follow based on the kind of reasoning patterns used (e.g., diagnosis); and
3. allows an overview of the problem in terms of the entire set(s) of concepts/objects required and the overall reasoning pattern that utilizes the concepts/objects.

Patterns

Christopher Alexander et al. are usually given credit for introducing the notion of "design patterns" in their book *A Pattern Language,* which describes the use of patterns in architecture (Alexander [1977]). The software community, especially the OO community, borrowed the idea of patterns and applied it (generally) to detailed descriptions of common activities required of objects. Patterns, however, exist at all levels of abstraction. In this book, we differentiate very high level patterns (domains) from very low level design patterns. For instance, the "composite pattern" (Gamma et al., 1995) composes objects into tree structures to represent part-whole hierarchies. A pattern is thus a "description of communicating objects and classes that are customized to solve a general design problem in a particular context" (Gamma et al., 1995). Firesmith and Eykholt (1995) define patterns as "any reusable architecture that experience has shown to solve a common problem in a specific context." (This definition is more global in intention, resembling a high-level framework rather than a low-level pattern). One of the most "cognitive" definitions of patterns is Riehle and Zullighoven's (1996) description of patterns as "abstractions from a concrete form which keep recurring in specific nonarbitrary contexts." A pattern usually has several essential elements: the pattern name, the problem to which it applies, the abstract solution, the context, constraints, and the consequences of applying the pattern (the results and tradeoffs). Continuing the dwelling example, table 1.2 illustrates an example of a pattern for entering the front door.

TABLE 1.2. Simplified Pattern
Pattern for opening front door

Context:	Human, house, door
Problem:	How to open front door.
Constraints:	Access to key, alarm status
Solution:	Insert key into lock. Turn key to the left, while holding doorknob....

TABLE 1.3. Examples of Design Patterns Associated with Sorting Mail

1. **Pattern for Reading zip codes**
2. **Pattern for Sorting by:**
   - post office
   - street address
   - zip code
3. **Pattern for Sizing of:**
   - envelopes
   - postcards
4. **Pattern for Determining Postage**
5. **Pattern for Handling Unreadable addresses**

Patterns are cognitive in the sense that humans often think in terms of patterns (Jackendoff, 1994). We recognize patterns and we match patterns on a daily basis. For instance, the design composition pattern represents a generic ability people have to place selected items in their environments into a part-whole structure.

Design patterns provide detailed, reusable and procedural descriptions of design activities that take place within a reasoning/problem-solving framework. Thus, design patterns can be applied to, and organized around, frameworks, as shown in the "sorting mail" example in table 1.3. In order to "instantiate" the sorting mail framework, design patterns, such as "reading zip codes", can be used to address the details of implementing the framework. Design patterns can be generic (as in the "composition" pattern), or specific, as in the example in Table 1.3, with accompanying advantages and disadvantages.

COGNITION SUMMARY

The notion and utilization of cognitive patterns is, in fact, part of the OO world today, beginning with the idea of objects themselves being promulgated as more cognitive than traditional approaches. Humans tend to think of their environment as containing objects with certain characteristics that can be manipulated. Cognitive patterns provide the context, the background, the organizing principles that allow individuals to structure and manage these complex objects.

The use of cognitive techniques in information technology is also not new (Andriole, 1995; Loucopoulos, 1992; Rasmussan et al., 1994) However, these techniques have been used primarily to address human factors, GUI design issues or knowledge-based systems. Increasingly, however, cognitive approaches are being applied to other aspects of information system development in an attempt to find innovative ways of dealing with the ongoing "software crisis."

Domains, frameworks, cognitive maps and design patterns all represent examples cognitive patterns. "Frameworks" are considered to be specific, context-driven examples of cognitive patterns called "domains." The term "cognitive map," representing a kind of framework, best describes the KADS Object approach presented in the remaining chapters. Design Patterns, detailed contextual descriptions of object behavior and communication, "instantiate" "frameworks," although in some respects, selected "patterns" can also be considered low-level frameworks. In other words, the distinguishing feature that differentiates one type of pattern from another is based on the level of abstraction. The extent to which a "domain" differs from a "design pattern" is dependent on the level of detail and specificity required.

THE RATIONALE FOR USING COGNITIVE PATTERNS

Overview of Cognitive Approach Benefits

The foregoing description may be intellectually intriguing, but in order to convince OO analysts and designers to learn yet another modeling technique, the authors must provide practical and important reasons for its use in order for a cognitive pattern approach to be considered helpful. A compelling case must be presented regarding the application of cognitive patterns to OO systems because intuitively we think that introducing yet another modeling technique increases our difficulties, rather than diminishing them.

Just as there is a search for the unified field theory in the hard sciences that would explain and reconcile other theories, there is a search within computer science for the one representation scheme that will mirror all aspects of reality.

Unfortunately there are many views of reality, and each model will reflect only selected aspects of some reality. It is probable that we will always require more than one model to obtain a holistic view of an organization or a process or a system, despite the problems associated with impedance mismatch and the maintenance of consistency among various views. The choice of views should be motivated by the particular system profile and constraints (e.g., database design may need to be data-centric). Eventually we may have access to metamodels, where each view is a kind of building block that fits with other views in a straightforward fashion. Each view then shows a particular frame of reference. A data view would provide one perspective; a business process view would provide another. As mentioned previously, a cognitive pattern view can identify and describe a perspective that reflects the reasoning/problem-solving activities of a system or organizational process. A cognitive pattern view can be used to model system and/or organizational processes because:

- the processes themselves are obviously based on reasoning/problem-solving activities, or
- the analyst/designer and/or the system stakeholder can understand the processes better when they are described in this manner.

For instance, a logistics process is primarily based on reasoning/problem-solving, whereas a payroll process is primarily concerned with posting and the calculation of relatively simple algorithms. However, an analyst may choose to model the payroll process as if it were based on more complex reasoning/problem-solving activities because the view helps clarify an issue, because it makes more sense to users when it is presented in such a fashion, or because it is the fastest way of identifying the objects required for a new payroll system. (It should be noted however, that the initial understanding of *how* a payroll process works is the result of a reasoning/problem-solving process).

The primary reasons for using cognitive patterns as a framework for object oriented projects are:

1. to successfully manage complexity;
2. to better identify the scope and boundaries of the proposed project and to provide a vocabulary by which the scope and boundaries can be discussed;
3. to quickly identify the necessary and sufficient object types required by the proposed project;
4. to emphasize, and incorporate, the role of knowledge within an organization; and

5. to enhance the consistency and validity of class design, and to enable novices to become quickly proficient at class design.

Each of these reasons is discussed below. Although subsequent chapters will discuss the KADS Object Framework in detail, a simple version of a KADS Object cognitive pattern called "Suitability Assessment" is introduced in figure 1.9 to assist in understanding the following sections.

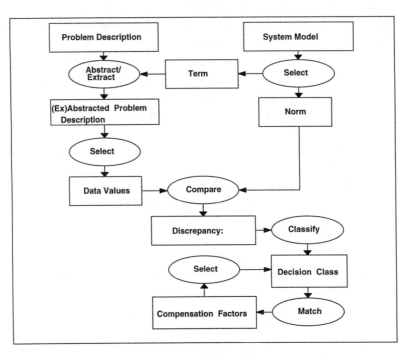

FIGURE 1.9. Suitability Assessment

Figure 1.10 illustrates a simplified example of this cognitive pattern that assumes the pattern is being applied to an insurance process. The rectangles predict the type of data/information required and the ovals predict the kind of collaborative operations or behavior that will use the data/information. The arrows reflect the general flow of reasoning. There is a tendency to read these patterns as data-flow diagrams. They are not data-flow diagrams, however; they represent the underlying reasoning pattern of a particular approach to solving problems. Suitability Assessment is a cognitive pattern which is used when a problem solver is attempting to make a decision, usually binary (e.g., "yes/no," "accept/reject"). A key ingredient of this model is that the decision can be changed based on com-

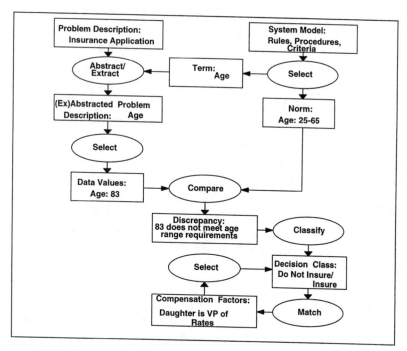

FIGURE 1.10. Suitability Assessment Example

pensating factors. It should be noted that the terms used to describe the rectangles and ovals are changed to reflect the type of information found within an actual project (e.g., a Suitability Assessment model in manufacturing will use different terms than the same model found in the health field). The project-specific terms, however, will have the same underlying meaning of the terms found in the basic pattern.

KADS Object consists of 21 of these cognitive patterns that represent frameworks for organizing and cognitively modeling one's environment (system processes, business processes).

Managing Complexity

A primary argument for applying cognitive patterns to OO projects is the need for analysts/designers to cope with increasing amounts of complexity in the projects in which they are involved. Systems are becoming more complex. Complexity is often defined formally as a function of the length of the shortest message conveying certain information, or the length of time it would take, at a minimum, for a standard universal computing machine to perform a particular task (Gell-Mann, 1995). Informally and intuitively, complexity is something we know we are experiencing when we feel overwhelmed and lost in the midst of a seemingly over-abundant amount of information, or when we struggle to grasp the interrelationships that exist within a system. The use of cognitive patterns presents a view of organizational or system processes that provides intellectual tractability by exploiting the reasoning/problem-solving aspects of the processes. For instance, if one of the processes of a project is identified as a Suitability Assessment pattern, the cognitive pattern for Suitability Assessment can be used as a template to structure and organize this particular process. (These cognitive pattern templates are discussed at length in chapter 2). The ability to apply these patterns at varying levels of abstraction is of great benefit, depending on the need of the analyst/designer. Cognitive patterns are generally applied at a very high macro-level (e.g., the patterns found in the finance process for a large, international firm) or at a somewhat lower level (e.g., the patterns associated with internet security activities). Because these patterns are cognitively based, we have an intuitive understanding of them. Hence, they contribute to comprehension, as opposed to creating yet more layers of confusion.

Determining Scope

Beginning with the premise that knowing the scope (an understanding of the desired functionality and boundaries) of a system is required to successfully develop a system, we can proceed to the question, "How is the scope obtained?" In small simple systems the scope is easy to grasp or can be explored by prototyping and user requirements. In medium to large systems, we enter the murky world of complexity where the scope is often vague and difficult to discern, and where user requirements are ill structured. Prototyping user requirements and use cases can assist in determining scope, but in our experience, prototyping user requirements, and use cases cannot serve as the sole determinants for scoping projects. It is not always clear what activities are within scope, because the original scoping document is not sufficiently clear and detailed. Prototyping can result in an endless process of scope creep with little functionality underlying screen design. After users have agreed to a screen design, implementing the underlying functionality can result in budget and schedule overruns, resulting in RAD (rapid application disasters). In addition, requirements change—a fact of life. A context is necessary in which to think, structure, evaluate and communicate about scope and modifications to scope. For instance, how does an analyst/ designer know what ramifications a proposed change may have to the existing scope? In addition, no consistent rigorous notation exists for communicating about scope. Scope and boundary statements are often narrative in form, with a laundry list of desirable features associated with the general goal of the project. The inability to associate these features with the work processes of individuals usually results in the automation of specific functionality rather than the more desirable state of automating a business process.

Cognitive patterns can be used to structure and provide the context for use cases, user requirements, to define scope and to serve as the vehicle of communication for stakeholders regarding scope modifications. In addition, the patterns can be nested (decomposed) to any desired level. For instance, the "compare" operation within the Suitability Assessment pattern has other cognitive patterns embedded within it; resembling the nested boxes shown in figure 1.11.

The modeling approach described herein, is used to provide a problem-solving, results-oriented, knowledge-using pattern based context for scoping projects. It is based on identifying, and cognitively modeling, the pertinent business patterns *within* which the project will take place, and then iteratively identifying and cognitively modeling the subpatterns that are included in the proposed system . The process of identifying and cognitively modeling the larger context, the patterns within which the project will take place, generally takes one to two days for large projects. Scoping needs to begin within a larger context than the actual project, so that it is evident what functionality/activities are to be included and what functionality/activities are to be excluded. Within a short period of time, the patterns that belong to the actual project are identified and cognitively modeled. Once this has been completed, user requirements and use cases can be tied

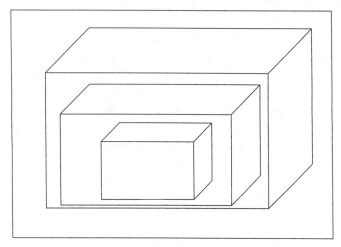

FIGURE 1.11. Embedded Models

to the patterns that represent the project processes. This is an iterative process and the patterns serve as the vehicle for discussions on scope changes. For instance, a pattern within scope might represent a process that makes a decision as to which statistical routine to use, given certain criteria and constraints. User requirements and use cases (e.g., default values to be automatically entered) are tied to the actual expected behavior of this pattern. For instance, in the Suitability Assessment model, user requirements and use cases would be attached to each oval (e.g., what does the user want to see when a "compare" operation is occurring? Who are the actors for this pattern?) When a scope change occurs with this process, it is evident which user requirements and use cases are affected. Conversely, a new user requirement can lead to the rethinking of scope.

In another example, a project's stakeholders provided a preliminary scoping statement regarding the need for a system to design parts for airplanes. Using the pattern approach, the processes that a designer uses to design parts were identified at a high level (e.g., "Decide which analysis programs will be used during the design" [Suitability Assessment pattern]). Using techniques described in chapter 3, the analyst would identify the patterns underlying each process and quickly modify the patterns for the particular project, using an iterative/incremental approach. These patterns are then used by the project stakeholders to decide which processes are within scope and to help define the boundaries. As the iterative/incremental project continues, these patterns are used as a vehicle for discussion regarding modifications to scope.

Identifying Objects and Object Behavior

Modeling of systems, particularly OO systems, has become a critical success factor. Modeling provides necessary information for implementors. It serves several purposes, but generally modeling is a way of displaying and structuring the object types that must be present, for example, in a system. The models also indicate object behavior, multiplicity, and relationships. With a few notable exceptions, the identification of the pertinent objects to be modeled is seen as a straightforward activity. One author suggests, for instance, that all one need do is find the "nouns" that exist within the organization and that these nouns then serve as potential objects for the system. Another author recommends finding the objects in documentation. With these ad-hoc approaches to identifying the object types that belong in a system/process, the specter of complexity and nonscalability appears. Perhaps finding the "nouns" for small systems is possible, but in our experience, finding and ensuring that the correct objects are available in large systems is a daunting task. In particular, when building large-scale OO enterprise models, the identification of core object types and the mapping of objects to business processes can be a formidable task, especially when the sources for objects are "nouns" and the reams of documentation that await the unwary. Use cases help identify objects. But in our experience, use cases need a context. Providing a context, such as a pattern, avoids use case issues such as excessive numbers of use cases and use cases at varying levels of abstraction.

Our ability to build enterprise-wide OO models in less than six months with fewer than eight FTEs (full-time equivalents) is based on our practice of applying cognitive patterns to scope and structure (i.e., provide a context for) business processes in such a way that the concepts (i.e., object types) and their behavior can be rapidly identified. The resulting models are then quickly and transparently mapped to any object-oriented notation. (The process of mapping from cognitive models to UML is discussed in detail in chapter 4). The cognitive models can be used at different levels of abstraction to identify:

- the global or core object types that are needed to support all business processes;
- the object types that are specific to a business process; or
- the object types that are specific to an application, and so forth.

By using the patterns as a knowledge-acquisition tool, the analyst/designer can structure the interviewing process to elicit specific object types and behavior associated with a particular pattern. Identifying the required object types, and associated behavior, becomes a relatively straightforward activity.

Incorporating Knowledge

Knowledge is defined as the expert use of data/information; in other words, an expert knows how to access data/information, knows where it is located, knows why it is needed and when it is needed. For example, in one situation a number of fabricators on a shop floor had varying degrees of success in fabricating an instrument. It was discovered during the modeling effort that although everyone used the same cognitive patterns, some individuals were experts and some were not. What then made some fabricators expert and others not? After modeling the patterns found in the processes they used, it was discovered that experts had more concepts available to them and also structured the concepts differently. In addition, a few nonexperts used different behavior than did the experts within the same pattern. The training manual was also modeled, which disclosed that the cognitive patterns existent in the training manual were significantly different than the patterns used by the fabricators. Upon completion of the modeling effort, it became possible to develop a "best practice" set of cognitive patterns for the shop floor, which meant that the expertise of the expert fabricators was incorporated into the methods used by all the fabricators. The cognitive patterns developed for the shop floor captured and represented the key knowledge that was now accessible to novices, where once it had only been available to a few talented individuals.

Every cognitive pattern has areas where expertise is particularly exhibited. For instance, a major source of expertise in the Suitability Assessment pattern is knowing what compensating factors to use to overturn a preliminary decision.

Knowledge can be communicated and distributed throughout an organization by the use of cognitive patterns.

Designing Object Classes

The mapping of framework pattern concepts and their behavior to object types and an object behavior notation results in a class design that is cognitively based. Use cases and design patterns are also tied to these patterns (discussed in later chapters). Because the mapping is relatively easy, a novice can be taught to do initial class design in a very short period of time. The initial mapping only includes domain (in the computer-science sense) object types, and through iteration and addition of nondomain-specific classes, the class design will be modified from its initial structure. However, all class designs reflect the underlying cognitive patterns on which they were based. It is then an easy task to determine why certain design decisions were made by accessing the cognitive pattern (design traceability). We have also found that class designers maintain greater consistency of design when cognitive patterns serve as the context.

REFERENCES

Alexander, Christopher, S. Ishikawa & M. Silverstein (1977). *A Pattern Language: Towns, Buildings, Construction.* NY: Oxford University Press.

Anderson, J.R. (1983). *The Architecture of Cognition.* Cambridge, MA: Harvard University Press.

Andriole, S.J. (1995). *Cognitive Systems Engineering for User-Computer Interface Design, Prototyping and Evaluation.* NY: Erlbaum.

Block, Ned (1990). "The computer model of the mind" in *Thinking: An Invitation to Cognitive Science, vol. 3*, D.N. Osherson and E.E. Smith, ed. Cambridge, MA: MIT Press.

Chomsky, N. (1980). *Rules and Representation.* NY: Columbia University Press.

Churchland, P.M. (1989). *A Neurocomputational Perspective: The Nature of Mind and the Structure of Science*. Cambridge, MA: MIT Press.

Cognitive Paradigms in Knowledge Organizations (Aug. 26–28, 1992). Second Intl. ISKO Conference, Madras, India.

de Champeaux, D., D. Lea & P. Faure (1993). *Object Oriented System Development*. Reading, MA: Addison-Wesley.

Fetzer, J., ed. (1992). *Epistemology and Cognition*, vol 6. Dordrecht: Kluwer Academic Publishers.

Firesmith, D. & E. Eykholt (1995). *Dictionary of Object Technology*. NY: SIGS Books.

Fodor, J. (1983). *The Modularity of the Mind*. Cambridge, MA: MIT Press.

Fodor, J. & Z. Pylyshyn (1988). "Connectionism and cognitive Architecture: a critical analysis." *Cognition*, 28, 3–71.

Gamma, E., R. Helm, R. Johnson & J. Vlissides (1995). *Design Patterns: Elements of Reusable Object Oriented Software*. Reading, MA: Addison-Wesley.

Gell-Mann, M. (1995). "What is complexity?" *Complexity*, 1:(1), 16–20.

Goldstein, K. & S. Blackman (1978). *Cognitive Style*. NY: Wiley & Sons.

Hashway, R.M. & L.I. Duke (1992). *Cognitive Styles: A Primer to the Literature*. NY: Mellon Press.

Herschfeld, L.A. & S.A. Gel, ed. (1994). *Mapping the Mind: Domain Specificity in Cognition and Culture*. London: Cambridge Press.

Hinton, G., ed. (1993). *Connectionist Symbol Processing*. Cambridge, MA: MIT/Elsevier Press.

Jackendoff, R. (1994). *Patterns in the Mind: Language and Human Nature*. NY: Basic Books.

Johnson-Laird, P.N. (1983). *Mental Models*. Cambridge, MA: Harvard University Press.

Lakoff, G. (1987). *Women, Fire and Dangerous Things*. Chicago: University of Chicago Press.

Lakoff, G. & M. Johnson (1980). *Metaphors We Live By*. Chicago: University of Chicago Press.

Lakoff, G. & M. Turner (1989). *More Than Cool Reason: The Power of Poetic Metaphor*. Chicago: University of Chicago Press.

Langacker, R. (1987). *Foundations of Cognitive Grammar, vol. 1: Theoretical Prerequisites*. Palo Alto: Stanford University Press.

Mayer, R., P. Benjamin, B. Caraway & M. Painter (1995). *A Framework and a Suite of Methods for Business Process Re-Engineering*. College Station, TX: Knowledge Based Systems.

Rasmussan, J., A. Pejtersen & L. Goodstein (1994). *Cognitive Systems Engineering*. NY: Wiley.

Riehle, Dirk & H. Zullighoven (1996). "Understanding and using patterns in software development" *Theory and Practice of Object Systems,* 2(1), 3–13.

Senge, Peter (1990). *The Fifth Discipline: The Art and Practice of the Learning Organization*. NY: Doubleday.

Wagman, Morton (1991). *Cognitive Science and Concepts of the Mind: Towards a General Theory of Human & Artificial Intelligence*. NY: Praeger.

Introduction to KADS Object

KADS OBJECT BACKGROUND

The cognitive pattern model presented in this book, KADS Object, is based upon a body of public-domain research that was conducted in Europe from 1985 to 1994, funded by the ESPRIT consortium. As such, it is nonproprietary. The methods resulting from this research initiative are referred to in the literature as KADS (*knowledge acquisition and design structure*) or CommonKADS. KADS was originally designed to serve as a methodology for the development of knowledge-based systems, and in Europe this is still a major focus. It is designed, in part, to facilitate the modeling of individual expertise. We have included numerous references to the published material on the KADS research initiatives (de Hoog et al., 1992; Wielinga et al., 1992), and will not attempt to provide further background on the basis or findings of the original KADS research efforts here. We encourage those interested in the research basis for KADS Object to refer to the many articles, papers, web sites and books on the subject (Tansley and Hayball, 1993; Hickman, 1991).

Description of KADS Object

KADS Object was created as an extension to KADS, to allow direct support for object-oriented decomposition and a greater inclusion of research on human cognition. Our experience with KADS Object has shown that the basic characteristics associated with knowledge and problem-solving at the person/individual level are also present at the business-process, system-process and enterprise level. KADS Object is a cognitive pattern modeling approach that views organizations, processes and systems as problem-solving, results-oriented, knowledge-using entities. As discussed previously, it is based on the assumption that human beings use a set of cognitive patterns with which to organize and filter their environment. In addition, because software products are created by humans, the underlying patterns embedded in software also reflect this problem-solving, results-oriented, knowledge-using view.

KADS Object has been applied successfully in four general areas:

- knowledge-based system modeling;
- as a cognitive pattern framework for OOA/D for system development;
- as a cognitive pattern framework for OO enterprise business process modeling (existing and redesign); and
- as a cognitive pattern framework for OO technical architecture modeling.

Other uses to which it has been applied (in a more limited fashion) include:

- specifications recovery (i.e., identifying the cognitive patterns embedded in nondocumented code and building a cognitive model representative of the code, which then provides a more generalized set of specifications);
- cognitive pattern modeling of existing training manuals, in order to compare training programs with existing best practices; and
- cognitive pattern modeling of packaged solutions (e.g., Oracle Forms) to identify the patterns found in Oracle Forms processes (e.g., shipping process), in order to compare them with an organization's similar process.

KADS Object is fundamentally different from data modeling, traditional enterprise modeling, process modeling and other modeling methods because it emphasizes the role of cognitive patterns. Specific techniques (covered in chapter 3) must be employed in order to elicit and model these cognitive patterns. The term "knowledge analysis" is used to describe the elicitation and modeling activities that are required to describe the problem-solving patterns used by individuals, organizations, systems, code or technical architecture (Gardner, 1995). Knowledge is defined as the application of human judgment to the *use* of data and information. This knowledge is often embedded in business rules.

Table 2.1 shows a relatively simple example of the differences between data, information and knowledge.

TABLE 2.1. Data, Information & Knowledge

Data	90, 81,110, 117	raw facts
Information	Q1 - $90,000, Q2 - $81,000, Q3 - $110,000, Q4 - $117,000	facts with a context
Knowledge	Retail sales figures are historically weak in the 2nd quarter, and stronger in the 3rd and 4th quarters.	Application of human judgment to the use of data information and knowledge.

As noted in chapter 1, KADS Object functions as an organizing structure and can be used effectively to:

- help identify the cognitive patterns being used by individuals, organizations, processes and/or systems to solve a problem, reach a conclusion or obtain a result (at any desired level of abstraction);
- provide a library of cognitive patterns, representing twenty-one distinct ways that humans structure their problem solving;
- identify the pertinent objects that are associated with identified cognitive patterns;
- help in the development of the object class design, with the cognitive pattern(s) serving as the "architectural blueprints" for the design; and
- provide a structure that enables elicitation of knowledge and definition of requirements.

There are two distinct groups of model deliverables in KADS Object: the KADS model and the Object model. The KADS model consists of four components: the concept descriptions, the pattern descriptions, the specific cognitive patterns (sometimes referred to as "problem-solving templates"), and the strategic description. These four components are interrelated and interdependent, and are collectively referred to as the "KADS Model." The Object model portion consists of an object model, mapped from the KADS model, and represented in the object notation of choice (map to UML.) The object model typically includes at least two major design elements: a static (object relationship) model, and dynamic (object behavior) models. Additional object notations can be developed from the KADS model, such as state-transition diagrams and use cases. The remainder of this chapter will focus on the KADS portion only. A full discussion of the techniques and mappings to the Object portion is presented in chapter 4.

OVERVIEW OF KADS OBJECT MODEL COMPONENTS

Figure 2.1 illustrates the four components comprising the KADS Object model and their relationships. The following discussion provides an introduction to each of the four components, followed by a more detailed explanation of each individual component.

The "Concept Description Component" identifies and structures all the concepts used in each and every cognitive pattern (called a "problem-solving template" in KADS literature), together with descriptions and definitions of the concepts. A concept is defined as an idea (e.g., world peace), a tangible thing (e.g., automobile), an intangible thing (e.g., unicorn), or an event (e.g., "end of month"). Concepts are the basic elements with which we think and reason. The concepts are grouped and structured according to relationships. These relationships are based on the role the concepts play in each pattern (problem-solving template). For instance, referencing the Suitability Assessment template shown in Chapter 1 (figure 1.9), the "compare" operation generally requires concepts found in the "data values" rectangle (known as a "role"), to be structured in "is_a" and "attribute" formats. The concept description reflects the content aspect of a cognitive pattern. The identical pattern (problem-solving template) will have entirely different concepts in different subject areas. For instance, as

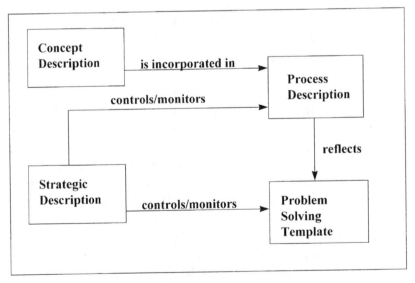

FIGURE 2.1. KADS Object Component

mentioned previously, the Suitability Assessment pattern (template) used in the insurance industry will incorporate concepts that vary from the concepts found in the same pattern used in manufacturing. Eventually these concepts will become the candidates for object types, object-type attributes and components (part-of) in the object portion of KADS Object.

The "Problem Solving Template Component "consists of a set of diagrams of the cognitive patterns used by a particular organization, process, system or individual. A library of templates exists consisting of twenty-one known patterns (included in Appendix A); but problem-solving templates can also be developed from scratch. The templates illustrate the underlying reasoning patterns used to solve a problem, reach a conclusion or obtain a result. A "reasoning pattern" is defined as a reusable interior-to-the-mind path that is used to draw conclusions, based on either an explicit or implicit understanding of the problem to be solved. Individuals tend to use the same reasoning pattern when similarities are found between the characteristics of an existing problem and one they solved in the past. A reasoning pattern is dynamic. The templates can be considered a kind of cognitive map, complete with landmarks, paths and goals/objectives, that help guide the problem solver through the reasoning path for a given situation. Problem-solving templates utilize specific subject area concepts that are required for successfully obtaining a result (e.g., solving a problem, reaching a conclusion). Once identified, these concepts are placed in the "concept description," which serves as a repository. The templates also show the operations that utilize the concepts, and which are required to meet the objectives of the template. (These operations, all of which have specific meanings [see Appendix B] will later serve as the source for object behavior). These concepts and operations, and their interactions, are described in detail in the "pattern descriptions" (one pattern description for each template). Problem-solving templates can be nested to any desirable level of abstraction (similar to data-flow diagrams). Each "operation/collaboration" within a template is a subpattern, with its own applicable problem-solving template. For instance, the "classify" operation in the Suitability Assessment template reflects the underlying presence of the "Classification" template.

The "Pattern Description Component" provides a textual explanation (with varying levels of detail) for the problem-solving template diagrams. There is thus a pattern description for each template model. A pattern description would, for instance, explain the precise role of specific concepts and detail the kind of operation/collaboration that will affect those concepts.

TABLE 2.2a. KADS Object Component Description

Model Component	Objective	Description
Concept Description Component	Construction of lexicon of concepts and their relationships	Definitions and hierarchical structuring based on role concepts play in each pattern/template
Pattern Description Component	Detailed textual description of each of the problem solving templates/patterns	Input concepts, output concepts (results),and the operations/collaborations manipulation the concepts for each pattern/template

TABLE 2.2b. KADS Object Component Description

Model Component	Objective	Description
Problem Solving Template/Pattern Component	Identification and modeling of the reasoning template/pattern(s) underlying each business or system or expert's process(s)	Predicts most important operations/collaborations and predicts role of concepts for each template/pattern
Strategic Component	Provide control information for relationships (e.g. sequencing) among and between patterns	Indicates any cognitive strategies which would be used to guide behavior of a set of patterns - strategies often modeled as a kind of meta pattern whose function is to control other patterns

The "Strategic Description Component" incorporates meta or control information that affects most, if not all, of the patterns. For instance, the strategic component could model and manage the business rules and logic that govern the sequencing of all pattern descriptions (and associated problem-solving template patterns). Table 2.2 includes a brief description and the objectives associated with each KADS Object model component.

Since the problem-solving templates and process descriptions can be nested to any desirable depth, KADS Object practitioners, and OO modelers in general, are often interested in access to guidelines (based on predefined criteria) that can be used to determine the optimal modeling depth. However, it remains a subjective evaluation: one should model to the level required to obtain under-standing, and to the level required by the organization's needs. Modeling for modeling's sake should be avoided.

The following section describes in detail the content and structure of the four KADS Object model components.

Concept Description Component

Key terminology

Concept

A concept is an idea or notion that we apply to the things, ideas or objects in our awareness. (Concepts will eventually be candidate object types/classes.) An object is anything to which a concept applies. It is an instance of a concept. For instance, the term "customer" is a concept. When a specific example exists (such as "cus-tomer Sam Smith"), an object is created that is an example of the concept "customer."

Hierarchy

A hierarchy is a grouping of concepts, bound together by a unifying relationship (i.e. "part-of," "is-a," attribute," "cause/effect," etc.)

As mentioned previously, the concept description component includes a description of the *pertinent* concepts required for each template pattern, the attrib-utes of the concepts (when appropriate), and the relationship that binds groups of concepts into hierarchies. Specific techniques are available to the knowledge ana-lyst for identifying and classifying concepts (discussed in chapter 3).

Also as mentioned previously, the concepts are placed into hierarchies based on a particular relationship in which the concepts will participate within a spe-cific problem-solving template. They represent a kind of building block that will serve as the source for building static object diagrams.

Table 2.3 shows examples of concept hierarchies, indicating the relationship described in each hierarchy. The notation used is a form of indentation. There are five major types of relationships used in KADS Object, as shown in the diagram: "part-of," "is-a," "caused-by" (i.e., cause/effect), "attribute", and "states_of". If desired, the number of possible relationships can be expanded, depending on the complexity of a process and its operations. Other relationships exist that are variations on the major five (e.g., "place-area" as a variant on "part-of"), or that

TABLE 2.3. Examples of Concept Hierarchies

Book (part of)	Title Table of Contents Chapters Bibliography
Library Furnishings (is a)	Bookshelf File Cabinet Chair Desk
Book (attribute)	Title Author Publisher Date of Publication
Library Furnishings (attribute)	ID Type Color Purpose
Book (states of)	Ordered In Stock Purchased
Book (is a)	Fiction Non-Fiction
Damaged Books (caused by)	Bindery Customer Librarian

reflect other associations (e.g., "followed-by"). Whether a particular concept participates for example, in a "part-of" hierarchy, is dependent on whether the operation/collaboration in which it is involved needs to view the concept in a "part-of" context.

As a general rule, concepts should not be modeled more than four levels (indentations) deep within a hierarchy. Since these hierarchies are mapped to an object structure, excessively deep hierarchies can result in excessively deep and overly complex object structures.

During knowledge elicitation and the construction of the concept description, redundant concepts are not only allowed, their identification is deemed an important activity. The more frequently a concept is used in diverse hierarchies and problem-solving templates, the more probable its core importance. Each time a concept is used in a hierarchy, and within a problem-solving template, it represents a different semantic context for that concept. For instance, the concept "water" has one implication when it is placed in a hierarchy called "Liquids" and quite another when it is placed in a hierarchy called "My favorite things."

The deliverable for the concept description component is a lexicon of the concepts: their hierarchical groupings, definitions and descriptions of the concepts, and an identification of the templates and roles within the templates in which the concepts are found (discussed later in this chapter). The extent to which this description is complete will depend on the extent to which the problem-solving template model and its associated pattern description are complete. In the typical iterative/incremental development environment, the first iteration will result in an incomplete KADS model.

Pattern Description Component

Key terminology

Pattern
A logical end-to-end sequence of steps (serial or parallel) that solve a problem, reach a conclusion, or obtain a result; each pattern is reflected by a problem-solving template(s). Patterns can be nested, resulting in subpatterns and sub-subpatterns, etc. Examples of business or system processes that are made up of various patterns and sub-patterns include: the accounts-payable process, the customer care process, developing a strategic plan, designing a database, designing an error report, invoicing a customer, and the database commit process. A pattern description is completed for each pattern and subpattern, and includes the goals and objectives of the pattern, the input into the pattern, the output of the pattern, and the operations/collaborations that result in the output.

Input
The concepts required to perform the operations of the pattern.

Output
The concepts, new and existing (with changed attributes and state changes) that result from the activities of the operations in a pattern.

Operation   A specific behavior (a cognitive step) within a pat-
                                 tern, (i.e., "match P.O. to invoice" is an example of
                                 an operation). Operations use concepts, where
                                 concepts are employed collaboratively to com-
                                 plete some behavior.

The first activity that occurs when beginning to build the Pattern Description
Component is an identification of the applicable processes (e.g., the sales/mar-
keting processes) and the probable level of abstraction that will be needed. The
second activity is to identify or construct (this topic is covered later in the book)
the patterns which underlie each process. All KADS model components undergo
multiple iterations and refinements in the course of knowledge elicitation/acqui-
sition and modeling, and the pattern description is no exception. Thus, it is important to communicate to the project sponsorship that processes and their
associated patterns identified early in the project are preliminary assessments,
and subject to revision as more is discovered about the project. Our experience
modeling at the enterprise level has shown that we might, for example, initially
identify six metaprocesses, and later revise that number upward or downward as
the modeling iterations progress. Processes can be metaprocesses (highest level
of abstraction for a given project), or processes (next level of abstraction from
meta), or subprocesses (next level of abstraction from process), or sub-sub-
processes, and so forth. Processes at the highest level have several patterns
embedded. Eventually (usually at the 2nd or 3rd level), one process equals one
pattern. Patterns are made up of individual operations; each operation is a potential subpattern or set of subsubpatterns. If an operation within a pattern is to be
modeled using a problem-solving template and a pattern description, then the
operation, by default, becomes a nested pattern. If the operation is merely
described as part of a pattern, it remains an operation. It is possible, if desired, to
decompose operations to any level of detail. Detailed operations, in our experience, are often equivalent to design patterns (ala Gamma).

Figure 2.2 illustrates a simple example of the spectrum of macro to micro
processes.

The following list is representative of typical candidate metaprocesses from
a telecommunications company. Each of these metaprocesses will have one or
more problem-solving templates associated with it, where the problem-solving
templates represent the reasoning pattern(s) that underlie each process.

1. Customer Operations Process
2. Order Fulfillment and Provisioning Process
3. Customer Fault and Repair Process

4. Billing and Payment Collection Process
5. Sales Process
6. Product Creation Process
7. Engineer Network Process
8. Procurement Process
9. Market Strategy Process

The templates reflecting these meta-processes were decomposed down three levels of abstraction for each process, which was determined to be the appropriate level of detail required by the client organization. This meant, for instance, the template for process #1 (customer operations), when decomposed, resulted in four subpatterns/subtemplates, and each of these four subpatterns resulted in three sub-sub-patterns. As mentioned previously, the candidates for decomposition/nesting are the operations found in each template pattern. The desired level of granularity for the problem-solving templates is directly proportional to the requirements of the stated goal.

The cognitive steps that an organization, expert or system uses to accomplish some result are not always available to the conscious mind, and can, in fact, be "compiled." A good example of compiled knowledge is your response when I ask you to describe how you tie your shoelaces. Although you have been tying your shoelaces for years, you will undoubtedly experience difficulties articulating the process. Thus obtaining the information needed to complete a problem-solving template pattern can require the use of knowledge-acquisition techniques designed to elicit compiled knowledge. (These techniques are covered in chapter 3).

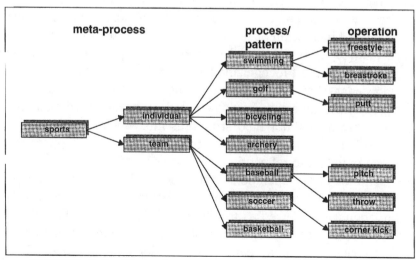

FIGURE 2.2. Meta-Process, Process, and Operation

Pattern Description Deliverable

Once the metapatterns have been identified/constructed, a description is begun for each pattern. The pattern description itself is a primary deliverable and includes the following:

- the goal/objective(s) of the pattern, the problem(s) it is designed to address;
- the input (in terms of concepts);
- the output (in terms of concepts, new and existing, their attributes and state changes);
- a concise, textual description of all operations (cognitive steps) that are needed to attain the goal/objective(s) of the pattern. Operations can be viewed as collaborative behavior that utilize n-number of concepts;
- an identification of any subpatterns that will need modeling; and
- any other pertinent information relating to the process (optional).

Usually, before the problem-solving templates associated with a process can be identified from the library of templates (or constructed), the pattern description must be at least partially completed. The pattern description (especially in terms of the operations and desired output) can be used to identify the appropriate template(s). However, as soon as there is a candidate problem-solving template, it can be used to help guide the development of the pattern description. The template can be used to elicit information about the pattern.

In one client engagement, a process was described in part and the template "heuristic diagnosis" was identified as the underlying problem-solving template pattern. However, according to the expert who was describing the process, his description did not include an operation that was expected by the template. The knowledge analysts believed that the operation in question was "compiled," resulting in the expert not recognizing its existence. Through the use of a specialized knowledge-elicitation technique, the operation was discovered and acknowledged by the expert. It should be noted, however, that the templates are to be used as templates, not rigid structures into which processes are shoehorned. As will be discussed later in this chapter, the templates must be expanded and modified to reflect the processes of interest.

The description of the operations in the pattern description can be relatively informal. Because of our requirement for flexibility in representation, a single representation language is viewed as too limiting. Therefore KADS Object avoids standardizing on a representation to describe the operations. Operations may be sequential, parallel, procedural, pattern driven, dependency driven. To a large extent, any description that accurately reflects cognitive steps, that makes sense to colleagues and users, and conveys *knowledge* of the pattern being modeled, is acceptable. The common goal of any process modeling approach ultimately is to comprehend the workings of the process under consideration.

The lack of a standard representation language for the pattern descriptions has been a criticism leveled against KADS in general. We hold what appears to be a minority viewpoint: that flexibility of notation for cognitive modeling is necessary, due to the variability of human cognition. Understanding that a price is paid for this flexibility, in our experience the benefits outweigh the disadvantages. On the other hand, there is no practical reason why a formal representation language could not be adopted (e.g., set-theoretic, fuzzy sets . . .), and certainly the KADS community in Europe has begun to address this issue (e.g., the CommonKADS workbench).

The mapping to an object notation occurs primarily based on the problem-solving templates (PST). The pattern descriptions eventually are saved as design artifacts, serving as the explanatory source of information and detailed knowledge represented in the PST. The PST model provides a more formalized language (the language of roles, operations and reasoning patterns) and can thus be verified and validated to a greater extent.

The deliverable for this component is a set of pattern descriptions, one for each process (meta and nested), completed to a level of detail that meets the need of the project or the time-boxed iterative/incremental effort.

Problem-Solving Template (PST)/Pattern Component

Key terminology

Problem-Solving Template/Pattern	A diagram illustrating the reasoning pattern that underlies each process and subprocess. The diagram is made up of two symbols—rectangles and ovals—with arrows showing the flow of reasoning. The rectangles refer to "roles" and the ovals to "operations/collaborations."
Operation	A collaborative or specific behavior (depending on whether the templates\patterns are reflecting meta/high-level processes or detailed subprocesses) within a problem-solving template, noted by the symbol of an oval.
Role	A named set of concepts that serves a specific purpose, or role, (either as an input or output) in a given operation, noted by the symbol of a rectangle.

Collaboration　　　　　　Two or more roles serving as input to a single operation in order to produce a desired output.

The "Problem-Solving Template" (PST) component is the heart of KADS Object and represents one of its most definitive features. The PSTs are cognitive models in the tradition of "domains," "frameworks" and "cognitive maps" discussed in the first chapter. They provide an organizing structure and context for each business or system process. Perhaps the greatest value in the PSTs with respect to modeling is their ability to predict problem-solving behaviors. This is enabled by the results of the KADS research, which delivered the twenty-one PSTs as a library of different problem-solving patterns.

PSTs are based on the premise that most basic human problem-solving strategies can be distilled to a set of generic models. For example, the diagnostic problem-solving template can be applied to diagnosing an infectious disease, diagnosing a problem afflicting your car transmission, or finding a bug in software, for each follows the same general problem-solving diagnostic pattern. The PSTs have been tested extensively in practice, and are generally very consistent in their mapping to problem solving across diverse domains.

Since the idea of problem-solving templates is generally a new idea for most people, it is important to find analogies that can help clarify the meaning. Table 2.4 shows an analogy between linguistics/language and the KADS models.

It is grammar (PST) that provides the structure to guide the usage of words (concept description) within sentences (pattern description), and the use of sentences within a larger context of dialog management. Dialog management (strategic description) addresses our expectations about appropriate responses to our words and sentences, and governs the proper sequencing of events. For instance, if two individuals engage in conversation and one asks the other "How are you?" the strategic model would suggest waiting for an appropriate response such as "I'm fine, thanks" before moving on to other topics.

It should be noted that the PSTs tend to map more closely to a process when applied to processes at a finer grain of detail. The KADS modeling techniques can be applied effectively at any desired level of abstraction; however, when modeling metaprocesses, the generic template models tend not to apply. Processes modeled at high levels of abstraction are made up of combinations of templates, as shown by the variety of output of a metaprocess. One of the outputs may be a "diagnosis," which would indicate that the "diagnostic" template is embedded within the metaprocess. Another output may be a "prediction," which implies the "prediction" template. As one "drills down" the processes, the library of problem-solving templates generally apply more directly.

TABLE 2.4. Analogy with language

KADS Object	analogous to	Language
Concept Description	=	Dictionary
Pattern Description	=	Sentences
PST/Pattern Model	=	Grammar
Strategic Description	=	Dialog Management

The PSTs emphasize the "what" rather than the "how" and do not, as a general rule, show iteration in the same sense that a traditional process or data-flow diagram would show iteration. Iteration is usually implied in the template, and made explicit in the process description.

PST Diagrams

The PST is a very simple model, and consists of only two symbols—a rectangle (the "role") and an oval (the "operation"). Each role can be considered a named set of concepts that will collaborate to perform some action and achieve some result (output). The operation (type of collaboration) will act on these concepts to achieve some result. Arrows are used to show the general flow of reasoning. There are a limited, defined number of roles that concepts can play within a given template and a limited, defined number of operations/collaborations that can occur in that same template. The operations/collaborations can be loosely defined as manipulations on sets of concepts. Operations reflect the variety of ways humans utilize and think about concepts.

Appendix B presents narrative definitions for selected roles and operations. The definitions for the operations are very fine grained and not all projects require such subtle differentiations (e.g., the operation "extract" is very similar to the operation "select"). See Tansley and Hayball (1993) for another approach to defining operations. Unless the modeling effort requires detailed and exact specifications for the operations, many of these operations can be used interchangeably. Depending on the needs of the analyst, the level of abstraction theoretically can be lowered to where each operation affects only one concept (very detailed and exact). However, since the problem-solving templates and pattern descriptions are generally used as *a source for the information needed to build object models,* it generally does not make much sense to model to a fine-grained level. Again it is the analyst/designer who makes the decision as to what level of abstraction will be the most helpful for a particular project.

Figure 2.3 shows a simple, nonexpanded example of a PST, which is the generic model for Systematic Diagnosis. For each "role" there will be a set of concepts that belong in that role. One of the tasks of the knowledge analyst is to identify which concepts belong in each role, and then place these concepts into hierarchical groupings based on the use of the concepts by the "operations." At a metaprocess level, the roles consist of the type of information required rather than detailed list of concepts. Until the patterns have been validated and nested, capturing detailed concepts is premature. An example of the type of information that is useful at a metaprocess level is the item "customer-profile information." This would contrast with the more detailed delineation of a list of customer-profile concepts. Other examples of types of information include "infectious-disease hypotheses," "equipment scheduling information," and "test suite repository."

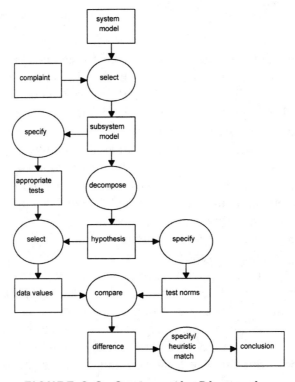

FIGURE 2.3. Systematic Diagnosis

Figure 2.4 illustrates an example of the type of information that might apply to the "Systematic Diagnosis" template. (Again, actual concepts would be identified after the appropriate types of information had been identified and validated.) The area of interest for this example is medical diagnosis. The basic reasoning flow is as follows: A *complaint* ("my foot hurts") is received by the physician (or system). Based on the nature of the complaint, a *subsystem model* (e.g., orthopedics) is selected from the *system model* (e.g., knowledge of the anatomy and physiology of the human body, presenting symptoms, range of hypotheses, appropriate tests, normative values, etc.). Incorporated into the subsystem model are the *hypotheses* and *tests* that are specific to orthopedics. Tests are run and *data values* are obtained, which are then compared to the *test norms* to arrive at a determination of the *differences*. (Note that the template does not address the actual running of the tests; if desired, that activity could be modeled using a different template). Based on the differences and the hypotheses that are supported by these findings, a *conclusion* (diagnosis) is reached.

This template represents one high-level model of how diagnosticians reason through to their conclusions. An example of expansion/modification to this PST might include identifying additional roles that would take the place of the gigantic

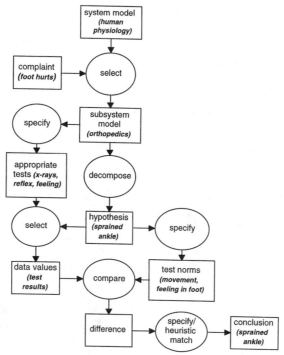

FIGURE 2.4. Systematic Diagnosis: Ankle Injury Example

system model, such as the addition of a role entitled "set of hypotheses" and a role entitled "set of tests." An example of a nested drill down might include the identification and modeling of the template(s)/pattern(s) that are embedded in the *specify/ heuristic match* operation.

Concept behavior can be seen as collaborative, where the emphasis is placed on identifying the total set of concepts contributing to a desired outcome. In addition, an assessment of *each* concept's contribution during a collaborative effort can be made (e.g., the contribution of the concept "joint mobility status" in the *specify/heuristic match* operation). Conversely, the specific behavior of a specific concept can be identified. It is fashionable to assume that only the latter example is worthwhile and purist OO. As mentioned previously, it is our belief that knowing how objects collaborate within a business (or system) process and their associated patterns, is essential to understanding the larger context of object behavior.

Figure 2.5 shows the same generic PST, "Systematic Diagnosis," applied to troubleshooting an electrical problem for a car.

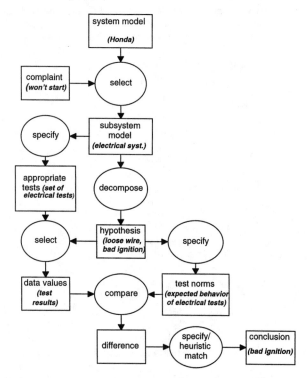

FIGURE 2.5. Systematic Diagnosis Car Problem Example

When first exposed to the notion of PSTs, there is often a tendency to read them as traditional process flows, flow charts, work-flow diagrams or data flows. However, PSTs do not fall neatly into any of these categories. The difference lies in the type of information being modeled within one template, which can include data flow, decisions, etc. Cognitive-modeling approaches tend to explore questions such as "What do you do next?"; "What do you do when you get confused?"; "Then what happens?"; "How do you make a decision?" rather than "What kind of data do you need, use, store?" or "Where do you send the results?" The answers to the last set of questions are important, but they are usually discovered as components of the answers to the former questions. (The answer to, "Then what happens?" may include a reference to the sending of a confirmation to another department.) Again, the emphasis in cognitive modeling is placed on the reasoning and problem solving that occurs in a process, not the document flow.

Each template from the library of templates exhibits not only a different configuration pattern of roles and operations, but the names given the roles and operations also vary. The names often reflect the area within which that particular template was first described (e.g., nuclear industry). Therefore, the names of the roles and operations must be changed to better reflect the project actually being modeled. Each library template's roles and operations have been defined and, if desired, the definitions can be represented using a formal language (e.g., set-theoretic). A glossary can be kept, if desired, that indicates the relationship between the names given the roles and operations for a project-specific template with the original names in the library templates. For instance, the generic KADS role "problem description" may be changed to "insurance application" for an insurance company. The generic KADS operation "compare" may be changed to "determine differences in residence address" for a mail list application.

PSTs are the flip side of the coin of the pattern descriptions. Pattern descriptions describe in some narrative detail what is happening in terms of the operations that are used in the templates. One should be able to look at the problem-solving template diagrams and find a more detailed explanation of the diagram in the pattern description. For instance, the operation "compare" found in a template can be described in the pattern description using a textual description, using set theory notation, using pseudo-code or some other notation. We have found that "use cases" (Jacobson, 1993) can be developed quickly and effectively when the templates are utilized to provide context and leveling for the use cases. The application of use cases is shown in the case study described in chapter 9.

Library of Problem Solving Templates

The library of twenty-one PSTs currently exists in the public domain, and represents the kernal of the KADS Object library. The templates are differentiated by the kind of solution provided by each template. Table 2.5 lists the twelve most common templates and the type of solution provided by each. Examples of these and other templates are included in Appendix A.

All templates in the KADS Object library are categorized as analysis-type templates or synthesis-type templates. Analysis-type templates are concerned with the manipulation of existing components (a closed-world scenario) within a particular template. Synthesis-type templates are concerned with the introduction of new elements (an open-world scenario) into a particular template. For instance, the "Systematic Diagnostic" problem-solving template is an analysis-type template. All of the possible diagnoses for broken bones are known. The "design" problem-solving template is a synthesis-type template. When designing a new chip, no knowledge exists of all of the possible solutions. Needless to say, synthesis-type templates tend to carry greater risk and tend to have increased complexity of implementation when contrasted with analysis-type templates.

The PSTs are regarded as minimalist blueprints, which undergo modification and refinement through multiple iterations of the model, incorporating feedback from subject-matter experts (SMEs) or other stakeholders. The minimalist blueprint metaphor works as follows. Imagine that you have decided to build a house. You purchase a software package, which includes generic blueprints, and which

TABLE 2.5. Library of PSTs

Problem Solving Templates	Solution Type Sought
1. *Analysis type*	*Concerned with existing components*
1.1 Classification	Placement into a category (solution)
1.2 Systematic Diagnosis	Cause (conclusion)
1.3 Heuristic Diagnosis	Cause (conclusion)
1.4 Assessment of Suitability	Decision
1.5 Monitoring	Difference
1.6 Prediction	Expected values
1.7 Repair	Remedy
2. *Synthesis type*	*Concerned with new components*
2.1 Planning	Sequence of actions
2.2 Design	New product/service/structure
2.3 Prediction	Expected behavior
2.4 Configuration	Assembly of components
2.5 Scheduling	Constraint satisfaction (time based)

allows you to first select the general type of structure that applies (e.g., house, factory, store). You select "house." The program then creates a generic blueprint of a predesigned house based on your selection. Upon reviewing the generic blueprint, you determine that your unique requirements require modifications to the design ("master bedroom too small," "need a storage room," and so forth). The blueprint is then modified to adjust to your family's specific needs. The key is that you did not initially select "factory" and then try to modify that generic design to create a house. You chose a preexisting "template" that closely matched your requirements, and from that developed an acceptable model with a minimum amount of effort. Modifying a PST generally means expanding it. Because the library templates represent the minimum "core" reasoning pattern, the PSTs developed for real projects tend to be twice the size (in terms of additional roles and operations) of the library templates. In addition, occasionally a different operation may be substituted for a library template operation.

In our experience, the library of twenty-one PSTs works much the same way with human problem solving, directly applying to >80% of the business and system processes we have modeled, assuming that we are modeling at a relatively detailed level. It is generally the case that individual templates tend to blur at higher levels of abstraction. When the level of abstraction is high (for instance, at the metaprocess level), templates reflecting the processes need to be built from scratch, recognizing that several library templates are likely to be "nested" within a single high-level abstraction. Rules for constructing problem-solving templates will be shown later in the chapter.

In figure 2.6, a fragment of a medium-level process called "Review Production Data" from a testing application is shown as an example indicating the presence of a nested template. A nested PST library template ("Suitability Assessment," indicated by the arrow) underlies the operation called "5.2 Review." "Suitability Assessment" is a template where the objective is to make a decision (often binary), based on an assessment of a difference. In this example, the "Suitability Assessment" template presented below is partial. (See Appendix A for complete diagram).

In some cases, a library PST may require so much modification that it loses any resemblance to its original, generic form. Typically, this indicates that the wrong PST has been selected, or it can indicate the need for a unique PST that does not yet exist in the KADS Object library. Construction of new PSTs specific to an organization can facilitate greater reusability. For instance, a new PST called "Maintenance" might be created by an organization, serving as a kind of generic view of how maintenance is handled for all departments. Table 2.6 shows the steps needed to build a PST from scratch. In order to construct a PST, the analyst/designer needs to begin developing a "pattern description." The first

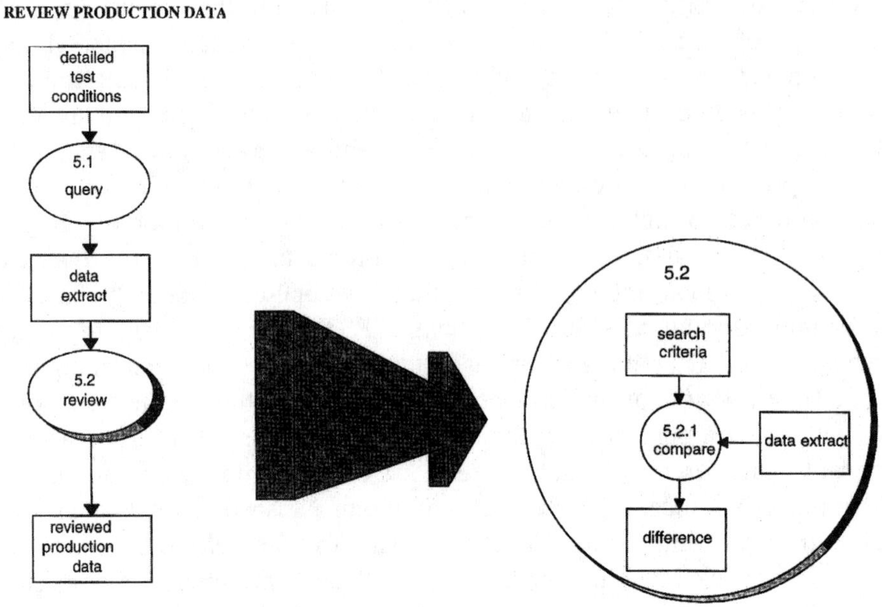

REVIEW PRODUCTION DATA

FIGURE 2.6. Nested Template Example

attempt at developing a pattern description with a SME(s) (subject-matter expert) should last no longer than an hour. This limitation keeps the analyst/designer and SME from going too deeply too fast.

The deliverable of this component consists of the set of problem-solving template (PST) pattern models and nested templates pattern for an area of interest, developed at a level sufficiently deep to satisfy the needs of the project.

Strategic Description Component

Key terminology

Strategy   The application of meta-level management/ control/planning functions that affect the ordering and dependencies of processes in the process descriptions and problem-solving templates

The Strategic Description Component provides a layer of overall management of the business logic that governs, for example, the sequencing of patterns. Not every project benefits from having a strategic description. Fine-grained and detailed processes that do not display many interdependencies, and can run from start to finish with readily available resources, may not require development of a strategic description. We typically include it when circumstances indicate a clear

TABLE 2.6. Steps for Building a PST

1. Identify high level meta process(es) of interest (e.g., the customer care meta process).

2. Determine purpose of process and desired output/result/conclusion for the process of interest. Using the Pattern Description format, begin filling out the major sections, starting with the output section. This is one of the most important steps; a good understanding of the output desired will prove of great assistence in identifying the patterns that underlie the process.

3. Determine the input requirements needed to obtain the desired output. Under what circumstances does the process begin? Begin with type of information required (e.g., "personnel records"), rather than specific concepts (e.g., "name").

4. Ask SMEs questions that refer to the order of, and explanations of, the operations; for instance, "what do you do first?", "then what happens?", "how do you usually solve that problem?", "why do you do [some activity]?". Elicit the general case and try to avoid detail. It should be clearly understood by participants and stakeholders whether the Pattern Description is being completed for an existing process, or for a future-as-we-would-like-it-to-be process. Operations can be compiled (ie hidden) in the minds of the SMEs. Specific techniques (described in Chapter 3) may need to be used to elicit the compiled operations. The existence of compiled operations is often discovered when there is no evidence of an operation that should exist, given the desired output.

5. Diagram a PST/pattern, based on your initial Pattern Description. Rectangles represent type of information (roles), and ovals represent the operations. Use nouns to refer to the roles, and verbs to refer to the operations. Modify until the SMEs are satisfied that the PST/pattern represents the process at a high level.

6. Determine whether any of the library PSTs/patterns are evident. Generally one or two outputs from an operation indicates the level at which the library templates begin to play a role. Identify any candidate library PSTs/patterns and validate with SMEs.

7. Modify the constructed PSTs/patterns and pattern descriptions to desired level of detail or until library PSTs/patterns occur. Identify the concepts that constitute the "type of information" previously gathered, and complete the concept description, pattern description, strategic description and finalize the PSTs/patterns.

8. Construct use cases for selected PSTs/patterns or operations within PSTs/patterns. (See Chapter 9 for information regarding the relationship of use cases to patterns).

business value. The contents of the description itself vary from project to project.

In some instances the strategic description has consisted of a template model that is a variant of the generic PST/pattern for "Monitoring." It can be used to evaluate expected versus real behavior of patterns. (Refer to Appendix A for a model of the "Monitoring" PST.) While it is true that the "Monitoring" template could be appended to each individual process, it may not be the most elegant solution for overall monitoring of all processes. By developing a global "Monitoring" PST at the strategic-description level, reusability is leveraged because the strategic description (like the concept description) cuts across all patterns and PSTs. In fact, the strategic description can utilize any format or approach that makes sense for a given project. For one engagement, the strategic description consisted of a diagram showing all the linkages between the patterns. In another project, it consisted of all the global business rules (business rules that impacted all processes).

In other situations, it has been used to differentiate sustaining processes from core processes, where sustaining templates/patterns are placed in the strategic description. A core process is a process that represents the work the corporation does in support of its mission. For example, a bank would have a core process regarding customer services. A sustaining process is a process that supports the core processes. An example of a sustaining process would be human resources. It, in itself, consists of a number of processes that may require modeling in the normal way, but through its services, it also impacts core processes such as customer service by ensuring that sufficient number of employees are hired and retained. In some instances, this differentiation varies, depending on how an organization perceives its processes.

Other uses of the strategic description include:

- Identifying and diagramming the linkages between the patterns where a pattern sends output to another pattern, receives it from another pattern, shares concepts with another pattern and so forth;
- Identifying specific strategies regarding the circumstances under which the order of the patterns is changed;
- Controlling the timing of patterns, especially in a real-time environment; and controlling exceptions/error handling that affect more than one pattern.

The strategic description deliverable is optional and the format is highly flexible, depending on the needs of a given project.

Selecting a Problem-Solving Template

The primary selection criteria for choosing a PST/Pattern is based on the kind of solution sought, which is precisely the type of problem solving reflected in the

"Suitability Assessment" PST. When the analyst is trying to ascertain which problem-solving template applies for a given process, the "Suitability Assessment" PST (consciously or unconsciously) is being used to do so (see Appendix A). When deciding which problem-solving template/pattern applies, the analyst must ask himself the following kinds of questions: Does a given process seek to make a decision ("Suitability Assessment" PST/Pattern), place something in a category ("Classification" PST/Pattern), diagnose a problem ("Diagnosis" PST/Pattern), configure a structure ("Configuration" PST/Pattern), or design a product ("Design" PST/Pattern)? If it is not clear which template underlies a process, developing (to a limited extent) the process pattern description, will indicate the type of solution sought (i.e., the output). This will help identify the underlying pattern. As mentioned previously, if there are several different kinds of solutions/results that are outcomes of a process, the chances are that you are working with a meta- or high-level process that has several library templates embedded within it.

As soon as a candidate PST/Pattern has been selected, the analyst begins working with the SME or user, employing the PST/Pattern as a knowledge-acquisition aid. The logic of the template is explored with the SME to ascertain the appropriateness of that particular template, and to determine the extent to which it requires modifying. Selecting the wrong template is not an earth-shattering event. For example, a novice modeler might initially select the generic "Suitability Assessment" PST/Pattern as a starting point. After extensive modification the modeler is satisfied that the PST/Pattern is accurate, but it now more closely resembles a "Prediction" PST! Obviously, starting with a prediction PST would have been the correct choice, and less work in the long run. As a practitioner gains experience using the templates, mistakes happen less often. Occasionally a practitioner may have insufficient information to establish the precise choice of PSTs/Patterns and may for a short while consider two or three PSTs/Patterns as candidates. With increasing information, one candidate PST is selected. It has been our experience, and that of our clients, that experienced modelers identify/develop/use similar or identical templates when modeling the same process.

Linking Problem-Solving Templates

PSTs/Patterns define processes at various levels of abstraction (i.e., meta-process, process, subprocess), where each process is modeled as a separate entity. However, in nearly all cases, PSTs are linked to each other across functional boundaries. For example, customer-service processes and their PSTs/Patterns, are generally linked to billing processes and technical-support processes. A customer complaint relating to a technical problem might be an input to both customer service and technical support. A customer complaint relating to a billing problem might be related to both customer service and technical support. Concepts and operations within a PST/Pattern that are related to another PST/Pattern are indicated by dashed lines as in Figure 2.7. Figure 2.7 shows a partial pattern (5.0) with relationships with a role in pattern 8 and an operation (7.4) in pattern 7. When relationships are many and/or complex, a table can be built to describe the relationships. This avoids "spaghetti lines" on drawings.

Conventions of Modeling Activity

A list of the diagrammatic conventions (Tansley & Hayball, 1993) that should be followed when constructing or modifying the templates is shown in table 2.7. We have added a few guidelines to Tansley's original list based on our experience. The guidelines are kept brief because the emphasis in KADS Object is on flexibility rather than on strict formalized methods.

Summary of Modeling Activity

The major activities associated with developing the KADS Object models are shown in table 2.8. Although the list is presented in a sequential format, many of the activities can, and should, be done in parallel.

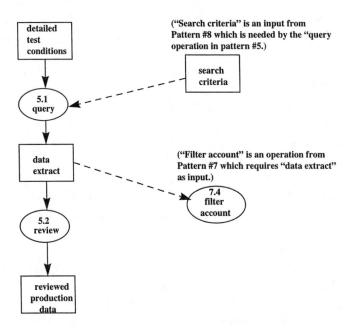

FIGURE 2.7. Linkages between PSTs

TABLE 2.7. Diagrammatic Conventions

1. Roles are represented as rectangles with their name inside (usually a noun).

2. Operations/collaborations are ovals with their name inside (usually a verb).

3. Possible directions of operations/collaborations are marked by one-way arrows.

4. An operation/collaboration generally represents a transformation of one or more roles into one or more new roles, in terms of the concepts "residing" in the roles.

5. No role may be directly connected to another role, and no operation/collaboration can be directly connected to another operation/collaboration.

6. Ovals with emboldened lines or which are shadowed indicate the presence of nested templates/patterns.

7. PSTs/patterns do not specify <u>how</u> nor <u>when</u> to perform the operations/collaborations.

8. Each PST/pattern should fit on a 8-1/2 x 11 sheet of paper for the sake of readability and ease of understanding. Diagrams too large to fit a single sheet should be abstracted up a level, and sub-patterns developed on separate sheets.

9. Almost any drawing tool can be used to manufacture the diagrams. We start off with hand drawn diagrams and then use "Topdown" to automate and store the diagrams. The European community has developed several tool kits which support KADS.

TABLE 2.8. Major Activities for Building KADS Models

1. Identify and describe the processes of interest (business or system) in terms of output/input/operations, at the appropriate level of abstraction (meta process, process). Followthe Pattern Description. format. This should be the first task of the analyst/designer.

2. Identify the type of information required, followed by a more detailed description of the concepts required. Structure the concepts hierarchically, according to relationship. Follow the Concept Description format.

3. Identify or construct PSTs/patterns based on the findings from the Pattern Description, modifying as appropriate. Follow the PST/Pattern diagram format.

4. Determine the need for a strategic description and construct if necessary. Allthough there is no specific Strategic Description format, generally examine the project to ascertain if a Monitoring (or other) PST/pattern would be an appropriate choice for a format.

5. Describe and/or diagram linkages between patterns, if desired, and decide whether the linkage model should "reside" in the Strategic Description. This is usually the last task of the analyst/designer as it requires information from the activities above.

REFERENCES

de Hoog, R., R. Martil, B. Wielinga, R. Taylor, C. Bright & W. van de Velde (1992). *The Common KADS Model Set.* KADS-II/WP 1-11/RR/UvA/018/4.0.

Gardner, K. (1995). *KADS Object Class Syllabus.* KPMG Peat Marwick LLP.

Jacobson, Ivar. *Object Oriented Software Engineering: A Use Case Approach.* Reading, MA: Addison Wesley, ACM Press.

Martin, James and J. Odell (1995). *Object Oriented Methods: a foundation.* Englewood Cliffs, NJ: Prentice-Hall.

Rumbaugh, J., M. Blaha, W. Premerlani, F. Eddy & W. Lorensen (1991). *Object Oriented Modeling and Design.* Englewood Cliffs, NJ: Prentice-Hall.

Tansley, D. & C. Hayball (1993). *Knowledge Based Systems Analysis and Design: A KADS Developer's Handbook.* Englewood Cliffs, NJ: Prentice-Hall.

Wielinga, B., W. van de Velde, G. Schreiber & H. Akkermans (1992). *The CommonKADS Framework for Knowledge Modelling.* KADS-II/T1.1/PP/UvA/35/1.0.

PART 2

KADS Object
Model Development

Summary

Part 2 consists of:
Chapter 3: Knowledge-Elicitation Techniques for Modeling Cognitive
          Templates/Patterns
Chapter 4: Mapping Cognitive Models to Objects
Chapter 5: Other Uses of KADS Object

These chapters include an introduction to specific techniques for development of KADS Object models, which go beyond simple interviewing techniques and explore proven methods for eliciting and validating deeply embedded knowledge. Detailed examples are provided for mapping components of KADS Object cognitive models over to object types, relationships, attributes and behaviors. Finally, diverse applications of cognitive modeling are discussed relating to BPR (Business Process Reengineering), knowledge management, development of user requirements, skills inventories, training development and more.

Objectives

The objectives of part 2 are:

- To delve deeper into the actual knowledge-elicitation and model-construction techniques of KADS Object.
- To demonstrate, by use of specific examples, the mapping of KADS model components to OO design elements such as object relationships, collaborations, behaviors and business logic.
- To explore the application of cognitive patterns to areas outside traditional OO analysis and design.

CHAPTER 3

Knowledge Elicitation Techniques for Cognitive Models

INTRODUCTION

In order to construct the KADS model, a variety of elicitation techniques are necessary. "Elicitation technique" is the term given any approach where the goal is to acquire information/knowledge from a person. There are a variety of elicitation techniques, ranging from simply asking questions to sophisticated software designed to "extract" the expertise from the expert. The techniques discussed in this chapter represent a selection from a larger set of cognitive techniques that are designed to elicit differing perspectives concerning information/knowledge. The results then are used to model some view or interpretation of reality. These techniques can potentially provide significant benefit to OO practitioners, particularly those interested in modeling cognitive patterns and/or gaining access to compiled knowledge. Just as electricians or carpenters use their expert judgment when deciding which tool to employ for a given task, OO practitioners can select the techniques they feel are most suitable for a project's goals and objectives. The more techniques available, the greater the range of elicitation problems that can be solved.

These techniques are integral to the field of knowledge analysis. The artificial-intelligence community pioneered the use of many of these approaches to elicit expertise for the purpose of designing and implementing knowledge-based systems. The term originally given this process of acquiring and modeling expertise was "knowledge engineering," but the word "engineering" is rather misleading. It implies operations on inert substances, as if attaining information and gathering facts were a kind of extraction or mining for gold ore from a passive source. "Knowledge analysis" is a more generic term, which broadly suggests an emphasis on the analysis effort that is involved. Acquisition of knowledge, information and data is more of a cooperative venture between the analyst and the expert/user/stakeholder than an engineering creation.

The use of these knowledge analysis techniques has been expanded, in this case into the realm of OO (object orientation), because of the desire to apply cognitive patterns to the modeling and construction of robust (and suitably documented) OO projects. Traditional techniques are not oriented toward the elicitation of cognitive material and thus cannot achieve the depth of understanding that is required to model cognitive patterns.

For example, interviewing, essential as it is to traditional system analysis, is a notoriously inadequate way of capturing information and user requirements; hence the importance given to prototyping for driving out user requirements. Interviewing is employed in knowledge analysis as well, but the intent and content of the interview differs (as will be discussed later in this chapter). In addition, interviewing is considered only one of the many approaches available to knowledge analysts.

It has been our experience that the techniques discussed below, when used to support modeling and prototyping:

- offer a superior method for understanding complex domains;
- help avoid the "if all you have is a hammer, than everything is viewed as a nail" syndrome (i.e., if interviewing is the only technique that is known, then it's used in every situation, whether it is appropriate or not);
- provide a range of approaches designed to elicit specific types of information/knowledge (e.g., compiled knowledge), giving the analyst more fine-grained tools than are traditionally available.

Table 3.1 presents a few of the more important distinctions that differentiate systems analysis from knowledge analysis.

"Knowledge analysis" is a component of the more extensive field of knowledge management. Knowledge management can be defined as the recognition of the importance of intellectual assets (e.g., employees' knowledge), the desire to manage these assets properly, and the understanding that so-called knowledge work is

TABLE 3.1. Comparison of Systems Analysis to Knowledge Analysis

Systems analysis emphasizes:	Knowledge analysis emphasizes:
User/stakeholder needs	• Experts' expertise <u>and</u> user/stakeholder needs
Procedural, process and factual data and information	• Emphasis on the cognitive use of data and information
Inputs, outputs and data flows	• Concepts and problem solving strategies
Quantitative data	• Heuristic, judgmental data
Structured/industrial engineering techniques	• Cognitive knowledge acquisition and analysis techniques
The syntactic aspects of the domain and its processes	• The semantic richness of the domain and the problem solving reasoning

ubiquitous in organizations. The topic of knowledge management is not within the scope of this book; however it provides the larger context for the subject of this book. The approach described herein fundamentally supports the wider vision of knowledge management because of the emphasis placed on viewing organizations/processes/systems from a problem-solving, knowledge-using perspective.

Figure 3.1 shows the desirable skill set for knowledge analysts, and as is evident, the attributes are similar to the characteristics required of competent system analysts.

However, few system analysts are asked to be intuitive, nor is the attribute "ability to think abstractly" generally listed as a desirable feature. However, the skill set needed by OO practitioners is almost identical to this list; and the addition of knowledge analysis skills can only enhance and deepen an OO practitioner's competence.

KNOWLEDGE ACQUISITION BOTTLENECK

One of the chief bottlenecks in the analysis and design of systems and processes is the knowledge acquisition problem. The reasons for this are diverse and include:

- our current understanding of the nature of expertise and knowledge is still rather rudimentary;

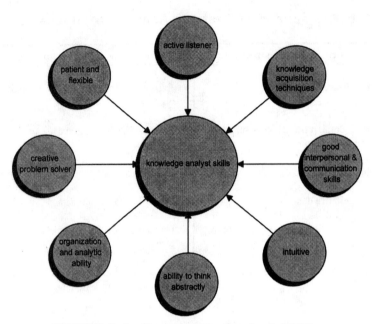

FIGURE 3.1. Knowledge Analyst Skills

- "in the box" thinking (inability to view a larger picture and/or insufficient creativity) by users/experts/stakeholders as well as by analysts, which inhibits creative brainstorming and differing perspectives. Certain cognitive characteristics of humans and their languages contribute to predicaments such as chronic miscommunication between users and IT staff, individuals' inability to verbalize accurately and coherently, individuals being unaware of the knowledge they possess (compiled knowledge), and the tendency people have to suppress uncertainty when asked their opinion. These problems hinder analysts' attempts to define user requirements, manage expectations and in general to obtain needed information;
- most analysts/designers have not been adequately trained in the variety of techniques available to them that can improve the quality of communication and assist in the acquisition of requisite information;
- the user/expert community may feel threatened, experience the time demands as excessive, and/or believe the effort is a waste of time, hence they become uncooperative.

Knowledge elicitation techniques can help reduce (but not solve) the problematic aspects of knowledge acquisition. A side benefit from the use of these techniques has been the enthusiasm many users/experts unexpectedly experience when participating in some of the cognitive knowledge acquisition techniques. From a subject-matter expert's perspective, knowledge acquisition can be an exciting and thought-provoking exercise.

KNOWLEDGE ELICITATION TECHNIQUES

Six techniques will be discussed in this chapter:

1. interviewing;
2. protocol analysis;
3. concept sorting;
4. scenarios;
5. observation;
6. event recall.

Each of these techniques is discussed below.

Interviewing

Interviewing is the most common and traditional method used for eliciting data and information, and it is an important technique for knowledge analysis as well.

However, it should be remembered that the interviewing process always results in incomplete information, no matter how frequently it is performed. Also the quality of the interview results varies widely. The quality of the results is a function of the interviewee's ability to understand and communicate, and the interviewer's ability to provide the appropriate context, to ask the right questions and to understand the answers. Skill at interviewing is rare: most analysts are given limited training and expected to develop expertise from experience. Unfortunately, learning often occurs at the expense of the user/expert/stakeholder.

From a cognitive point of view, interviewing is perceived as having two almost mutually exclusive objectives: obtaining facts and attaining understanding. Interviewing, as it is practiced in the system-analysis community, is oriented primarily toward obtaining facts. Unfortunately, facts are often sought before understanding is attained. In an effort to develop systems faster and faster, the analyst seeks facts to serve as the basis for coding and prototyping. The importance of gaining understanding before obtaining facts is a well-known precept of the ethnographer (someone who studies living cultures), and the OO practitioner would do well to study the techniques of the ethnographers. Ethnographers are aware that it is essential to establish a rapport with the interviewee, to understand his/her concerns and the context in which he lives and works. Trust must be developed, for example, before an individual will talk factually and candidly about how he prepares a certain tincture. The ability to read body language is considered a critical factor for successful interviewing.

The premature rush to facts (and to code) often obscures issues, which, had they surfaced earlier, would have saved developers from having to address these same issues at the more complex, detailed level. For instance, in the rush to get a system out as soon as possible, the underlying business needs may not be examined adequately, leading to yet another failed or compromised system.

When understanding is the goal, *unstructured* interviews are preferred. During this phase, very high-level and general questions are asked in order that the analyst can familiarize herself with the view of the user/expert/stakeholder and begin to appreciate the context of the project. Examples of questions asked at this phase include:

- What are the expectations regarding this project?
- What problem(s) is it going to solve?
- What is the role of this system?
- What constitutes expertise in this domain?
- What are your major concerns/issues regarding this project?
- How does the proposed project impact your current work patterns?

Once a baseline understanding is achieved *focused* interviews can take place, where the emphasis is on asking open questions that revolve around topics. Examples of topics include:

- Identification of major processes and patterns;
- Preliminary assessment of level of abstraction required;
- High-level use cases for patterns;
- High-level specifications/constraints for proposed system;
- High-level information on existing system (if project is to replace or modify existing system);
- High-level information on interface requirements with other systems.

Structured interviews are used to delve more deeply into details. The term "structured" refers to the presence of a format or organization, designed to elicit precise facts. Structured interviews do not consist of random questions, and are not meant to support "design by enumeration." Examples of the types of questions that would be asked at this level include:

- Can you describe what exactly is going on in this "compare" operation?
- Does this template reflect the kind of problem solving you do? If not, where do we need to make changes?
- Can you identify the concepts that belong in this "problem description" role?
- What are the necessary inputs for this process?

As mentioned previously, KADS Object can fit within existing methodologies, as it is a modeling view rather than a complete methodology. (KADS in Europe is used more as a life-cycle methodology). In some instances a methodology may call for user workshops in place of individual interviews. The same principles apply.

The advantages of interviewing are appreciable. Interviewing (when done well) can establish a rapport between the analyst and the user/expert/stakeholder, and is an essential part of information gathering. The disadvantages, however, are significant. There is always bias and error in verbal data (i.e., report may not reflect true behavior), and interviews *always* result in incomplete information.

INTERVIEW TYPES: EXAMPLES OF USE

1. **Unstructured**: to gain an understanding of the situation/ problem/scope;

2. **Focused**: to identify metaprocesses and preliminarily identify candidate problem-solving templates (PST);

3. **Structured**: to evaluate the relevance of a specific PST for a given process; to identify the contents of a PST's operations and roles; to complete the process descriptions.

Protocol Analysis

Protocol analysis is a technique designed to elicit very detailed information regarding a particular process (e.g., diagnosing printer problems). It is usually

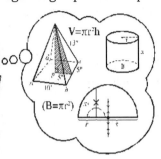

applied at a subprocess level, but can be used at any level of abstraction, depending on the complexity of the process. Complex processes need to be decomposed into subprocesses because the amount of detail provided by the protocol analysis can be overwhelming. The user/expert/stakeholder is asked to keep in mind three questions as he completes the process:

1. What are my goals for this process?
2. What are my methods for this process?
3. What am I seeing at any given time concerning this process?

He is then asked to complete the process, and while doing so, to think aloud. The interviewer often videotapes or audiotapes the session for review with the user/expert/stakeholder at a later date. The interviewer is responsible for identifying the principle utterances, or those comments judged most relevant, given the objectives of the session. Protocol analyses are unsurpassed for obtaining detailed information on difficult, primarily linear and complex processes. Actions taken during the process are explained and justified.

Considerable research exists showing the efficaciousness of protocol analyses (Newell & Simon,1982). The advantages include a lack of delay between performing the task and reporting on it; a detailed level of analysis is provided; incomplete information can be identified; and it is not subject to the bias of memory. The disadvantages include the fact that it is most applicable for linear and stepwise activities and human activities are not always linear; it is difficult for some users/experts/stakeholders to perform; and it can be time consuming and expensive. However, its use can avoid the thrashing that occurs among analysts/developers when there is insufficient information available to them, and it can clarify complex processes. We have found it to be invaluable and have used it in a variety of settings: to discover how an engineer designs an airplane part, to analyze workflow, to better understand a rating process, and to determine how an expert reengineers code.

A partial example of a protocol analysis is shown in the following example.

This is a transcript of an expert horticulturist describing his process of diagnosing the cause of leaves that show evidence of burning. Examples of his "goal, method and what am I seeing" statements are indicated.

- "People generally bring me leaves, like these, as symptoms. My objective is to identify the cause of the symptoms [GOAL]. I do this by looking at the samples that are brought to me and trying to develop a precise description of the symptoms [METHOD]. These leaves show evidence of burning, as indicated by brown areas [WHAT IS BEING SEEN AT ANY GIVEN TIME]. I first determine where the burning is located.
- If the leaf has a marginal burning or a killing of the tissues around the older leaves, this is evidence of salt damage; excess salt. This can occur for a variety of reasons; two most common. First is from too much fertilizer and the second is from improper leaching of the soil. Nothing else causes this kind of burning, so when you see it, you know for sure that it is caused by excess salt. Now this leaf shows no evidence of marginal burning, but rather burning between the veins.
- Burning of the tissues between the veins is caused by sunburn. This is very common. The first symptom is leaves that have become colorless like this one and this is followed by a killing of the tissues resulting in either a bleaching of the leaf or a browning of the whole leaf. Sunburn is a response to excess sunshine, but it really isn't caused by the sun so much as it is caused by the plant being too dry. . . . Plants that don't get enough water are susceptible to sunburn. There is one other reason why a plant might sunburn easily. Not enough iron. This is common."

PROTOCOL ANALYSIS: EXAMPLES OF USES

- To complete pattern descriptions and to identify patterns used by expert
- To obtain detailed information in order to construct or modify a problem-solving template
- To identify concepts required for the problem-solving template

Concept Sorting

Concept sorting is the process of identifying and structuring concepts and their relationships in a specified domain. The intent is to discover how experts/users/stakeholders understand and manipulate the concepts in their environment. For instance, the analyst may be interested in identifying the concepts that play a role in the "Systems Diagnosis" PST, as perceived by a specific subject-area expert. Also of interest to the analyst is the discovery of how the expert organizes or structures these concepts.

The analyst identifies a number of concepts that he or she believes play a role in a certain template, such as the "Systems Diagnosis" PST. Each candidate concept (e.g., "symptom," "blood panel") is written on a 3x5 card. A user (or expert or other stakeholder) is asked to group these cards (usually about fifty cards are provided at a time) according to any criteria they wish to use. In our experience, the vast majority of groupings turn out to be loosely hierarchical or, more rarely, the groupings resemble a semantic net. Redundant concept cards are not only permitted, they are encouraged. A concept that is used repeatedly in different groups is usually an important core concept. For example, in one concept-sorting exercise, the concept "customer" occurred twelve times. Each time it was used, it played a different role, such as "customer as purchaser" and "customer as complainer." In this instance, from an OO perspective, different roles, states or attributes of the object type "customer" were being identified.

After the individual has completed the groupings, the analyst asks questions concerning the placement of the cards, the shape (bell-shaped vs. localized groupings), and the meanings associated with the particular placement and spread. In our experience, this grouping remains relatively stable throughout numerous iterations. Generally, at the completion of this technique, either a quick sketch is composed or a polaroid picture is taken of the grouping.

Concept sorting possesses several distinct advantages. It is an ideal way, and the quickest way, for the analyst to become familiar with the landscape of a strange domain. The grouped concepts allow a rapid survey of the structure of the area of interest, as well as providing an expeditious way to bring recent arrivals to the project team up to speed regarding the subject matter of the project.

Based on our experience, individuals with similar levels of experience will develop comparable models. It is sometimes worthwhile to compare the concept groupings of experts with novices. Figure 3.2 shows two concept sortings of identical concepts, showing the differences between an expert's point of view

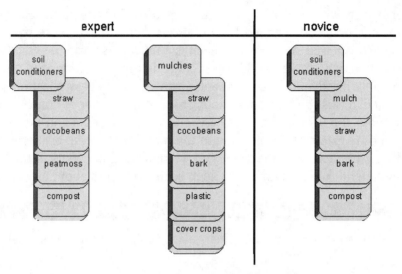

FIGURE 3.2. Concept Sorting

and the perspective of a recently hired entry-level trainee. In this example, an expert horticulturist was given a number of cards with concepts relating to soil conditioners and mulches. The expert differentiated between soil conditioners and mulch, whereas the novice placed mulch as a kind of soil conditioner. In addition, the expert identified some concepts that were missing (e.g., plastic, cover crops and peat moss) that the novice failed to identify. The results of such a comparison can be used to educate novices and significantly decrease the learning curve. (As an aside, this approach has been used to explain OO concepts to novices).

This technique also allows identification of incomplete information. Experts can readily identify the concepts that are missing when they examine the groupings of cards, as well as recognizing concepts that do not belong.

The expert/user/stakeholder groupings may or may not resemble the hierarchies the analyst has developed for the problem-solving templates. If they do not, the concept-sorting exercise can be used to explore the reasons for the differences. Usually, the differences exist because of the varying objectives of each. An expert's grouping reflects the way he or she has organized the concepts in order to most effectively use them during problem solving. An analyst's grouping reflects his understanding that these concepts represent the candidate object types and function as building blocks for the mapping to an object notation. The analyst is always free to utilize the expert's arrangement of concepts, but a price is paid during implementation if the expert's concept relationships do not map isomorphically to the relationships supported by OO notations. However, any concept hierarchies developed by the analyst must make sense to the expert (e.g., "beech is:a tree" is correct, "beech is:a flower" is wrong), even if they are not congruent with the expert's way of viewing and structuring the concepts.

The only disadvantage of concept sorting is the excessive number of concepts that can exist in large domains. A prodigious number of concept cards can stupefy both the user and the analyst. However, concepts can be categorized into groups (e.g., concepts referring to the rating part of the billing process), or level of abstraction (e.g., the twenty most important concepts in the organization). A general rule of thumb is to keep each session to about fifty cards.

CONCEPT SORTING: EXAMPLE OF USES

1. To identify concepts and their relationships required by specific PSTs;

2. To identify the expert/stakeholders' view of relevant concepts and their structure;

3. To identify missing concepts;

4. To understand the domain of interest.

Scenarios

Scenarios are test cases developed for either a simulated or natural environment where a person(s) or process or prototype completes a task or solves a problem.

Scenarios have a greater context and complexity than is generally found in the usual test data. Scenarios include most, if not all, the processes identified for a specific project. Scenarios are presented to the individual, process or prototype, and the results are analyzed. Scenarios can be designed to cover a range of difficulty and a variety of types of problems. Our experience has been that scenarios are best applied to tough or salient problems, problems at the edge of the domain, or problems with varying degrees of uncertainty. This use of scenarios is broader in scope than UML's (Unified Modeling Language) use of scenarios.

Scenarios have been constructed for a variety of domains: to test a patent application process with several possible show-stopper issues, to investigate the design of an engine cowl subject to severe environmental constraints, and to determine the best mix of chemicals given shortages of certain ingredients. An example of a lengthy scenario was a scenario that was developed to incorporate a set of very rigid, and conflicting requirements for designing engine cowls. Given this set of requirements, the expert(s) were asked to design the engine cowl. The purpose of this scenario was to determine the tradeoffs that were made in the design, since all the requirements could not be met satisfactorily.

The primary advantage of scenarios is its ability to identify the extent of brittleness and the boundaries of expertise of a process, or of a prototype, along a continuum of problem types. In addition, it is based on realistic problem solving, and does not rely on a person's memory.

However, scenarios have two disadvantages: they must be developed with care (it is important to design scenarios to obtain the kind of output desired), and the deliverables can result in an overwhelming amount of detail that requires careful interpretation. Also the tendency to use the scenarios to design systems to handle exceptions rather than the general case must be controlled.

SCENARIOS: EXAMPLES OF USES

1. To help complete pattern description(s);

2. To show a "thread" that cycles through most, if not all, processes and problem-solving templates of a project, with an emphasis on discovering the brittle components;

3. To understand how an expert(s) solves difficult problems or how the expert handles exceptions.

Observation

Observation is the act of viewing an individual while she is solving a problem or performing a task(s) in a simulated or realistic environment. Observation can be unobtrusive or obtrusive. If unobtrusive, the analyst watches, takes notes or videotapes without any interruption. "Obtrusive" refers to the agreement reached with the observed person that the analyst can interrupt and ask questions during the observation period.

Observation is a particularly good technique when the analyst is interested in discovering how and why a person makes a judgment or decision. It is particularly helpful for the Systematic Diagnosis, Heuristic Diagnostic, and the "Modification" problem-solving templates. Watching a diagnostician diagnose the cause of equipment failure, and then the methods she uses to fix the problem, can lead to a greater comprehension of the process than can be acquired during interviewing. If it is videotaped, the analyst can later review the tape with the person observed. It has been our experience that obtrusive observation is not as valuable as unobtrusive observation, because the asking of questions during the activity is generally disconcerting to the person doing the work. The flow of reasoning is impeded.

The major advantage of the observation technique is that it allows the analyst to actually experience the observed person's daily functioning rather than hearing the person's verbal report of it.

Not all activities warrant observation. Obviously the person must be performing task(s) that indicate that decisions are being made, and the discovery of these decisions must be considered important by the analyst. Observation can be used for a single pattern or a sequence of patterns.

Observation cannot show the reasons for the decisions. These must be obtained during the discussion following the observation. In addition, the Hawthorne Effect can negatively impact the results. The "Hawthorne Effect" refers to the phenomenon associated with watched behavior, where the behavior changes in response to the knowledge that someone is watching.

OBSERVATION: EXAMPLES OF USE:

1. To help complete pattern descriptions;

2. To help construct or modify problem-solving templates.

Event Recall

Event recall is a situation where an individual recalls past situations he has experienced. This approach is particularly useful for unusual situations that are often well remembered. It is especially good for attaining understanding, although it can be used to gather facts. For example, the analyst, having developed a good rapport and a trusting relationship with the user/expert/stakeholder, can ask such questions as: "What was the most difficult network you ever had to engineer?"; "What made it so difficult?"; "If you had it to do over again, what would you change?"

Event recall is not well suited to asking questions regarding daily or routine activities. Research indicates that individuals have a tendency to reconstruct memories rather than actually remembering them unless the memories are out-standing for some reason. Reconstructed memories are subject to error and bias and cannot be relied upon.

EVENT RECALL: EXAMPLES OF USES:

1. To gain a better understanding of the difficulties that could be encountered in a pattern;

2. To help complete a pattern description where the purpose is to establish the extent to which the process is brittle, and to identify the boundaries of the process in terms of unsolvable problems.

TECHNIQUES SUMMARY

A number of knowledge elicitation techniques have been presented that belong in every OO practitioner's tool kit. Their use can substantially enrich the quality of the information obtained from experts/users/stakeholders, and their use is necessary to construct KADS Object models.

Techniques designed to elicit cognitive material have been well discussed in the knowledge-acquisition literature and the reader is referred to these articles and books for further information on these and other techniques (Ericsson & Simon, 1984; Gardner, 1996; Newell & Simon, 1972; Scott, Clayton & Gibson, 1991).

REFERENCES

Ericsson, K.A., and H.A. Simon (1984). *Protocol Analysis: Verbal Reports as Data.* Cambridge, MA : MIT Press.

Gardner, K. (1996). *KADS Object Class Syllabus.*

Newell, A. & H. Simon (1982). *Human Problem Solving.* Englewood Cliffs, NJ: Prentice-Hall.

Scott, A.C. , J.E. Clayton & E. Gibson (1991). *A Practical Guide to Knowledge Acquisition.* Reading, MA: Addison-Wesley Publishing Co.

CHAPTER 4

Mapping Cognitive Patterns to Objects

MAPPING TO OBJECTS OVERVIEW

The concepts, relationships and behaviors expressed in the KADS Model can be mapped effectively to any OO notation. We have used different OO notations in client project work including Martin and Odell, OMT, Shlaer/Mellor, and most recently Unified Modeling Language (UML). The one constant in our engagement work has been a mapping of KADS patterns to Martin and Odell's "Object Event Schema" (Martin & Odell, 1995). The analogous model representation in UML is referred to as the Activity Diagram. These views show end-to-end processing and collaboration among objects at a high level. We have used Intellicorp's animated CASE tool LiveModel to test the logic of the event schemas. It is our belief that objects must be related to business processes. When objects are not tied to business processes, they are often disembodied from the realities of the business, and thus fail to meet the needs of the entire business. We are aware that this is a somewhat controversial belief, but based on our experience, disembodied objects do not contribute as much value as do objects that are based on processes. A common critique of entity relationship enterprise models has been that they frequently are of limited use, because they can be so removed from the dynamics of the business. It is true that processes can change over time, but the object model should be an organic structure responsive to the inevitable change that occurs in organizations. For instance, the notion of "customer" is perceived differently by different processes and these views should be accounted for in the object model. New products may be released by an organization that change the view of a customer as seen by selected processes. We are not suggesting a chaotic object model, but we are emphasizing the flexibility and adaptability that comes *with associating objects with business processes.* Processes (business and system) exist at varying levels of abstraction and each process is made up of sets of collaborating objects. Hence, a diagram that shows this kind of collaboration at the process level is invaluable.

For the purpose of the following discussion, the assumption is made that readers are generally familiar with object constructs. The emphasis is on the mapping activities rather than the actual construction of complete static and dynamic object models. Chapter 9 provides a case study using KADS Object, showing the actual construction of complete object models.

A typical scenario follows: When the KADS models have been completed to the degree desired, the initial action is the mapping of the concept description (the concept hierarchies) to an object-oriented static model. This is followed by a mapping of the template and pattern description operations to object behavior. Because the construction of the models takes place in an iterative/incremental development cycle, the initial modeling will be incomplete. For the first iteration, the decision can be made to develop KADS Object models and OO models in depth for one pattern, or a time-boxed approach can be used to develop as much of the models as possible for all relevant patterns. The time-box period usually ranges from four to sixteen weeks, depending on the size and complexity of the project, and usually includes a prototyping effort. Prototyping aids in driving out user requirements and testing the efficacy of the models. Based on the findings from the prototype effort (also time-boxed), the models are modified and expanded. This continues until the project is completed (again, usually within a time-boxed framework). The iterative/incremental approach to developing systems has its own set of issues (e.g., scope creep), but we believe it is currently the best approach given competing needs (e.g., time to market vs. quality of system, rapid deployment vs. adequate modeling and documentation).

As is probably evident, we consider an extremist RAD approach (rapid application development) to the development of OO systems to be shortsighted. Without sufficient modeling and an underlying application architecture, a system developed with tools designed to produce systems literally overnight results in the same stovepipe applications and inflexible systems that have haunted organizations for years. Maintenance becomes a nightmare and reusability an impossibility. While recognizing the need for organizations to move quickly, a reasoned approach that attempts to balance the competing needs (e.g., speed vs. the requirement for a robust infrastructure to support the development effort) works the most successfully.

MAPPING CONCEPTS TO OBJECTS: OVERVIEW

The hierarchies that have been constructed for the KADS Concept Description are made up of domain concepts, the presence of which have been proven to be necessary to successfully complete the pattern (e.g., solve the problem, make the decision or reach the conclusion). The decision as to which hierarchies should be developed, the identification of the relationship expressed by each hierarchy, and the determination of which concepts should be placed in the hierarchies is dependent on the requirements of the template in which the concept(s) play a role . In addition, the expert's way of structuring the concepts and the area in which it is being used also affect decisions about hierarchies. For example, the role "complaint," found in the "Systematic Diagnosis" template would require various symptom concept hierarchies. The actual contents and organization of these hierarchies would depend on the expert and the degree of discrimination required. A family practitioner may have needs for hierarchies dealing with common complaints such as "sore throat," whereas a specialist gastroenterologist physician might require hierarchies that refer to specific locations of stomach pain. These concept hierarchies serve as candidates for object classes (i.e., object types), object components, and object attributes. Thus the concept description (one for each pattern) is the primary source for the static object diagram.

Object behavior is obtained through two complementary KADS sources: the Problem-Solving templates (specifically the "operations"), and the Pattern Descriptions (specifically the detailed "operations"). Object behavior can be viewed from two perspectives:

1. collaborative (i.e., the totality of the contribution of all pertinent object type behavior to a template "operation" such as "match"), or;
2. specific (i.e., the behavior of a particular object type).

Collaborative behavior can exist at several levels: It can reflect the behavior of a single template "operation," or it can reflect the behavior of an entire pattern or series of patterns. Knowledge of collaborative behavior assists the designer in understanding the flow of a process, and/or a thread of execution and it can help structure testing and performance analysis.

If the Strategic Description has been created using problem-solving templates, its concepts and operations would be mapped as above. In any case, no matter what role the Strategic Description plays, its contents would be mapped to object types and/or behavior.

Mapping Examples: KADS Models

The examples used in this chapter are simplified examples (chapter 9 illustrates a real-world case study in some detail) of models developed for a system to diagnosis problems afflicting plants. The first activity for this particular engagement (as is true for all engagements) was to identify the processes. In this case a single broad, high-level pattern (Systematic Diagnosis) was used to reflect the diagnostic process. Based on this single metapattern, two subpatterns are shown for the purpose of this chapter. The problem-solving template for the diagnostic pattern is shown in figure 4.1, and the associated pattern description is shown in table 4.1. The first subpattern is based on the "select subsystem model" operation from the metapattern, and the second subpattern is based on the "specify appropriate tests" operation from the metapattern. These are shown respectively

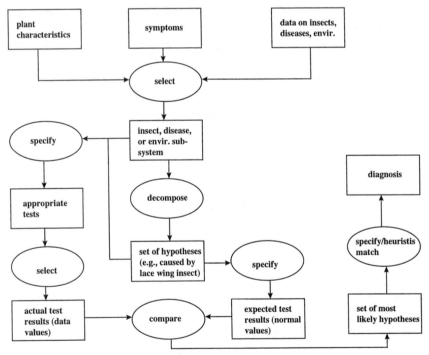

FIGURE 4.1. Systematic Diagnosis

in figure 4.2 and figure 4.3, with their associated pattern descriptions shown in table 4.2 and table 4.3. Figure 4.2 is a Classification pattern and figure 4.3 is also a Classification pattern, although the Suitability Assessment pattern is a possible candidate template.

Several concept hierarchies developed from these patterns are shown in table 4-4.

At least one concept hierarchy exists for every "role" in each of the templates. Generally, however, "roles" include more than one hierarchy. The number of concept hierarchies found in a "role" is determined by the needs of the "operation" that will act upon that specific role.

As was discussed earlier, redundant use of concepts during knowledge acquisition is encouraged, because it enables the analyst/designer to understand all the various ways in which the concept is used during the problem-solving process. Therefore, any concept may appear more than once in several different hierarchies within a problem-solving template, and may also occur in other prob-

TABLE 4.1. Pattern Description for
Plant-Problem–Diagnosis Metaprocess

INPUT:

1) Symptoms
2) Data on plant characteristics
3) Data on insects, diseases and environment
4) Insect, disease or environment "subsystem"
5) Appropriate tests
6) Actual test results (data values)
7) Set of hypotheses
8) Expected test results (data values)
9) Set of most likely hypotheses

OUTPUT:
1) Diagnosis

OPERATIONS:
1) *Select* applicable subsystem (insect, disease or environment), using knowledge of plant characteristics, and knowledge of insects/diseases/environment, based on presenting symptoms/evidence.
2) *Specify* the appropriate tests to be used, given the selected subsystem model and the set of hypotheses
3) *Decompose* the set of possible hypotheses from the selected subsystem model.
4) *Select* actual test results (data values) and *specify* the expected test values.
5) *Compare* the actual test results and the expected test values, and based on outcome, determine set of most likely hypotheses.
6) *Specify or heuristic match* the diagnosis.

TABLE 4.2. Process Description for "Select Subsystem" Subprocess

INPUT:

1) Symptoms (presenting) {attribute}
2) Insect, disease and environmental data
3) Plant characteristics data
4) Symptom subsystem classification criteria

OUTPUT:

1) Classified symptoms (subsystem)

OPERATIONS:

1) *Describe* the presenting symptoms of the plant, using knowledge of plant characteristics and knowledge regarding insects, diseases and environmental factors.
2) *Classify* the described symptoms, using the symptom subsystem classification criteria, to one of three subsystem categories: insect, disease or environmental causes. The criteria includes the list of possible symptoms, matched with insect, disease or environmental causes.

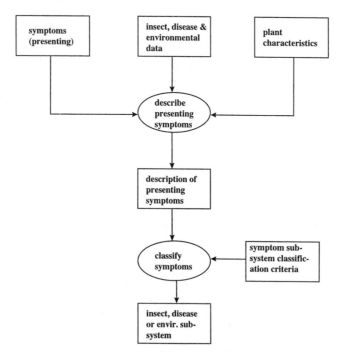

FIGURE 4.2. "Select Subsystem" Subprocess

TABLE 4.3. Process Description for
"Specify Appropriate Tests" Subprocess

INPUT:

1) Subsystem) {is-a}
    Insect
    Disease
    Environmental
2) Set of diagnostic tests
3) Set of subsystem hypotheses
4) Subsystem test set
5) Appropriateness criteria (attribute)

OUTPUT:

1) Appropriate tests

OPERATIONS:

1) *Identify* the tests that belong with a specific subsystem category (e.g., insect), from the set of all possible diagnostic tests, based on the set of hypotheses to be tested for the specific subsystem.

2) *Determine* appropriate tests to be run from the set of subsystem tests, based on the hypotheses (subsystem specific) to be examined and appropriateness criteria.

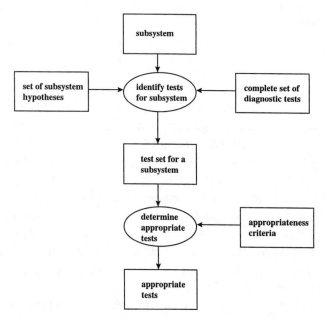

FIGURE 4.3. "Specify Appropriate Tests" Subprocess

TABLE 4.4. Selected Concept Hierarchies

1) Insects (is-a)
   - Chewing insects
     - Weevils
       - Root
       - Wood
   - Sucking insects
     - Scale

2) Diseases (is-a)
   - Fungus
     - Leaf spot
     - Rust
     - Leaf gall

3) Fungus diseases (caused-by)
   - Leaf spot
     - C. handilli
     - E. concentrica
   - Rust
     - P. vaccini

4) Symptoms (attribute)
   - Leaf
     - Yellowed borders on leaves
     - Burnt edges on leaves

5) Subsystem (is-a)
   - Insect
   - Disease
   - Environment

6) Plant (part-of)
   - Leaf
   - Root
   - Stem
   - Flower

7) Environmental factors (attribute)
   - Drainage:
   - Location:
   - Soil pH:

lem-solving templates as well. In the sample hierarchies above, the concept "insect" appears two times: once as the name of an "is-a" hierarchy entitled "Insects," and second as an entry under an "is-a" hierarchy entitled "Subsystem." Other possible hierarchies where the concept "insect" might appear include a "part-of" hierarchy that describe the various parts of an insect, and an "attribute" hierarchy that describes the attributes of insects (e.g., number of wings).

When the concept hierarchies are mapped to an object notation, the concept only appears once as an object type. However, the analyst/designer can use the information regarding the presence of redundant concepts to identify required attributes, relationships, methods and messages. For instance, the redundant concept "insect" could occur as a object type with attributes attached; it could also belong to a supertype called "Subsystem."

A particular hierarchy has a specific relationship (e.g., is-a) because an analyst/designer has determined that the operation that will be manipulating the

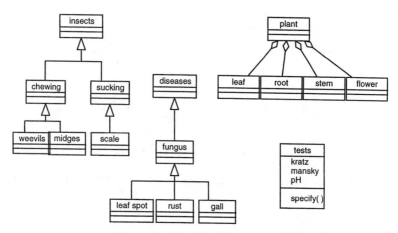

FIGURE 4.4. Object Model Example

concepts needs to view the concepts from that perspective. The hierarchies serve as basic building blocks that will be used to construct an object model. Hierarchies are similar to the pieces that make up the components of a Lego set. The pieces (the hierarchies) can be used to build various structures (object class design), each piece playing a specific role in the structure.

Mapping Examples: Object Model (Static Model)

The first step in the mapping of KADS models is to consider the concepts found in the hierarchies as candidates for object types and their attributes. We generally begin by assuming that all top-level concepts of "is-a" hierarchies (i.e., the "name" or root node of a hierarchy) are candidate object types, and all the indented member concepts that make up the hierarchy are candidate subtypes. This is followed by a mapping of the "part-of" concept hierarchies to object component structures. This is completed for each process. Figure 4.4 illustrates the results of the initial mapping of selected hierarchies from table 4.4. Initially all "is-a" and "part-of" hierarchies are mapped, with the understanding that during refinement, some hierarchies may be subsumed into other hierarchies.

While any object notation can be used, the examples are shown in the UML notation, using the Rational Rose Case Tool. The case tool will eventually build a composite object model from the concept hierarchies input from all of the KADS processes/templates. As the hierarchies from all the processes are mapped into the case tool, the tool communicates redundancies to the analyst/designer.

After the "is-a" and "part-of" hierarchies have been mapped, the "attribute" hierarchies are either:

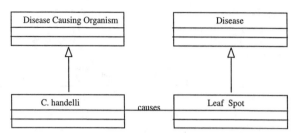

FIGURE 4.5. Relationship Example

• assigned to appropriate "is-a" hierarchies as properties of that supertype or subtype;
• themselves subtyped; or
• become associations between object types.

The choice is a design decision, based on the application architecture, performance objectives, the development environment requirements, and so forth. The appropriate *role of attributes* in a particular project is one of the more interesting decisions that class designers must make. These decisions are also based on answers to such questions as, "Is the attribute shared by more than one object type?" and "Does the attribute itself have properties?" For instance, if an attribute hierarchy is more than two levels deep, an argument can be made for subtyping it (e.g., the attribute "color" has a property of "degree of saturation" and it is "degree of saturation" that will hold a value).

Cause-effect hierarchies are not mapped to object types as these kind of hierarchies represent a kind of relationship that holds between classes. Usually the concepts found in "cause-effect" hierarchies are present in "is-a" hierarchies as well. The "cause-effect" hierarchies show the relationship holding between, say, two "is-a" hierarchies. For instance, a hierarchy may exist that expresses facts such *as "C. handelli* causes leaf spot." This association can be modeled in object notation in several ways. For instance, as shown in figure 4.5, *C. handelli* could be a subtype of a supertype entitled "Disease-Causing Organism," with leaf spot being a possible subtype of the class "Diseases," or the relationship could be expressed in an association called "caused-by" existing between the "disease object type" and the "organism object type."

At this point each of the hierarchies exists in isolation from each other. The building blocks (the hierarchies) are now ready to be combined into larger and more coherent structures. The analyst/designer must begin to make decisions concerning the structure of the integrated class design based on the KADS models and the purpose of the proposed project.

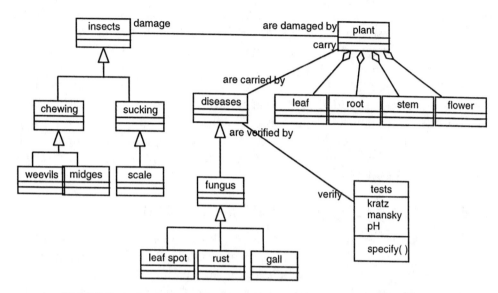

FIGURE 4.6. Object Model Example with Associations

After the hierarchies have been mapped to an object notation, the analyst/designer begins to assemble the object types into a class design, where some concept hierarchies may participate in an extensive inheritance structure, while others may have relatively flat structures. The analyst/designer determines the relationships and required multiplicity, resulting in a product such as the one shown in figure 4.6. The information needed to complete these class design activities can be found in the pattern descriptions and problem-solving templates, depending on the level of detail present in these two sources. Relationships can be recognized by the associations between and among concepts shown in the templates. For instance, potential relationships exist between the concepts found within the "appropriate tests" role and the concepts found within the "test norms" role within the "Systematic Diagnosis" template (figure 4.1). Conversely, "test norms" could become an attribute of "appropriate tests." Potential relationships also exist between the "data values" role and the "test norms" role, because each role participates in the "compare" operations.

Because the multiplicity is generally not explicitly described in the pattern descriptions, SMEs may need to be involved in this determination. Depending on the extent to which the modeling has been completed, relationships and multiplicity can also be explored and developed during prototyping.

The resulting object model, the first cut at class design, directly reflects the problem-solving templates in which the hierarchies originated. Over time, the class design will be iteratively refined, nonbusiness-specific classes will be added, and the design may require some changes to optimize performance. In our experience, however, the underlying cognitive structure of the PSTs remains the foundation of the class design.

Nonbusiness-specific object types and classes (e.g., application and implementation) are usually added to the object model after the mapping of the business concepts to objects. Examples of nondomain and lower-level object types/classes that can be incorporated into the object model, depending on the needs of the project, include: "GUI widget," "message processor," "message request," and so forth.

MAPPING EXAMPLES: OBJECT BEHAVIOR (DYNAMIC MODEL)

Object behavior is identified using the pattern descriptions and the templates. The analyst/designer has two options (not mutually exclusive) for documenting further detail within the pattern descriptions. The high-level pattern descriptions can incorporate more textual detail in the operations section. A second option is to describe a subpattern by nesting a template operation (as discussed in chapter 2). For example, the highest level pattern in the plant-problem–diagnosis system has seven operations, each a candidate for a subpattern. However, not every operation requires nesting; some operations are sufficiently trivial that modeling them as subpatterns contributes little or no value. For instance, the "select" operation affecting the "Data Values" role in the "Systematic Diagnosis" template is a relatively simple procedure that rarely requires a subpattern. Nesting should only be done to help clarify a pattern and to manage the complexity of an operation. Eventually, the operations could theoretically be nested to a level where only one concept is affected by one operation (i.e., a method). This is not recommended as a general rule. Chief among the issues is that the resulting extensive documentation becomes burdensome. The KADS Object models should serve as a major source of information for individual class behavior, but the OO notations (e.g., interaction diagrams) should be used to formally model it.

In many instances, each template is first transformed into an event schema, preferably using a CASE tool or drawing tool. Figure 4.7 shows the event schema associated with the "Systematic Diagnosis" pattern.

Each rounded rectangle in the "Event Schema" diagram represents an operation found in the problem-solving template. Note that the existence of nested-event schemas within the high-level event schema (similar to nested PSTs) is indicated by shading top-level operations. Also note that input variables (object types) and output variables (object types) are indicated near the rounded operations. The arrows refer to messaging requirements. For the highest level diagrams, messages are described showing which objects will need to collaborate to achieve the results of the operation to which the arrow points (destination).

At lower levels, messages can be described for individual object types. The triangle shown in Figure 4.7 refers to a control condition that notates and describes a requirement regarding some condition that must occur (in addition to the completion of the source operation) before continuing. Control conditions are described using if/then/else rules. In the example in figure 4.7, the triangle indicates that both operations must complete before continuing.

Event-schema diagrams are unique to Martin and Odell's OOIE notation, and although many CASE tools support it, there are several that do not. It is also important to note that the event schema is being incorporated into the UML notation in the form of Activity Diagram. Again note in figure 4.7 that each template operation is shown as an operation in the event schema, where each operation in the event schema represents a collaboration of n-number of objects, which are identified as input and output variables. The resulting model is then animated and tested logically to determine if the underlying class design (which was previously entered into the CASE tool) supports the collaborations. Once congruence between the object model and event schema is obtained, other more detailed behavior diagrams can be completed.

A sequence diagram (formerly referred to in OMT as a "message trace") is useful for showing the specific interactions between classes. The information needed to complete a sequence diagram can be found in the detailed pattern descriptions, template models and use cases that have been developed. The

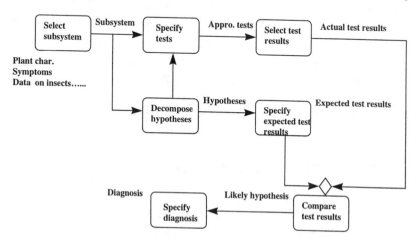

FIGURE 4.7. Event Schema for the Plant-Diagnosis Process

higher-level pattern descriptions/templates contribute to the development of sequence diagrams by illustrating which object types/classes are closely associated, and indicating which object types/classes would benefit from being presented in such a format. It should be noted that for large systems, the activity of creating sequence diagrams that incorporate many classes can easily become overwhelming; and reams of diagrams are often produced that are difficult to relate to one another. Figure 4.8 shows a sequence diagram for the plant-problem–diagnostic system where the information needed to complete the sequence diagram is found in the problem description (see table 4.1).

In addition to sequence diagrams, other behavioral diagrams such as collaboration diagrams, event flow diagrams, and state diagrams can be developed based on the information specified in the pattern description and template models. Figure 4.9 below is an example of a collaboration-diagram view of the sequence diagram in figure 4.8.

It is important to remember that the pattern descriptions and problem-solving templates at a high level of abstraction provide the *framework, context and organizing structure* for developing sequence diagrams, event-flow diagrams, state diagrams and use cases. Depending on the extent to which the templates/pattern descriptions are nested and detailed, the specific information needed to develop thorough sequence diagrams, event-flow diagrams and state diagrams may or may not be present in the KADS models.

Business rules are often identified as part of the activity of describing the patterns. Depending on the project and the object notation, these business rules may become objects themselves, or they may be modeled as constraints affecting object behavior. Chapter 9 covers this topic in more detail.

Design patterns can be used to further detail operations. A repository of reusable patterns can also be associated with either templates or with operations within templates. For instance, any "select" operation could have several design patterns associated with it, including a design pattern that defines how a "select" operation works.

For the examples shown in this chapter, a strategic description was not required and so is not discussed.

SUMMARY OF OO MAPPING ACTIVITIES

A KADS template representing the process by which the KADS models is mapped to an object notation is shown in figure 4.10.

The associated description for mapping to objects from a template is as follows:

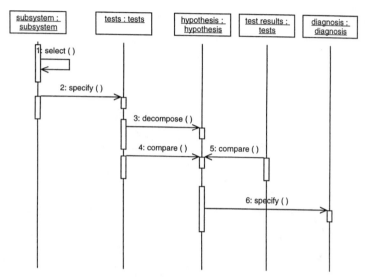

FIGURE 4.8. Sequence Diagram Example

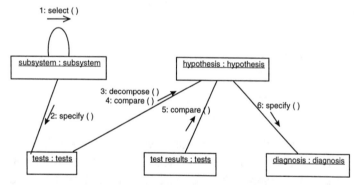

FIGURE 4.9. Collaboration Diagram Example

1.0 **_Map_** concept hierarchies (concept description) to object types *for each pattern*

> **1.1.** Begin mapping the "is-a" hierarchies (as supertypes/subtypes), followed by the "part-of" hierarchies (as compositions/aggregations).

> **1.2.** Decide whether "attribute" hierarchies will become attributes of an "is-a" hierarchy, be subtyped or be expressed as associations.

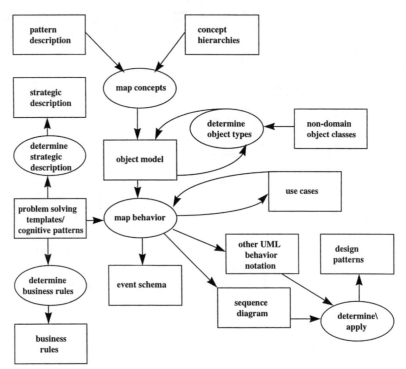

FIGURE 4.10. Object Mapping PST

1.3 Decide whether "caused-by" hierarchies will be expressed as attributes or associations.

1.4 If other relationships exist (e.g., "followed-by"), decide whether relationship will be expressed as attributes, associations, subtypes or other relationship supported by a particular OO notation.

1.5 Construct and refine the static object diagram, using the pattern description and problem-solving template model to identify and clarify associations and multiplicity. A static-object model is built for each pattern. Generally one object model is automatically created from the multiple object diagrams by the Case tool.

2.0 ***Determine*** extent to which nonbusiness object types/classes need to be incorporated, based on goals and objectives of the project. (Usually nonbusiness object types/classes are incorporated after the initial mapping model has been logically tested, and are generally not included as part of an object business model.)

3.0 ***Map*** behavior from pattern description and problem-solving template to event schema (or equivalent) for high-level, collaborative view, and to other UML supported notations for more detailed views.

    3.1 Map behavior that is concept- (object-type) specific to sequence diagrams or state transition diagrams (or equivalent), based on information found in pattern description and problem-solving template model.

    3.2 Map use cases to problem-solving templates or to individual operations. (This option is described more fully in chapter 9.)

4.0 ***Determine*** how business rules are going to be incorporated: as objects, as constraints on objects, as controls over object behavior. The decision may be driven by choice of object notation.

5.0 ***Determine*** how the strategic description is to be mapped, if a need has been identified for the existence of a strategic description. Depending on the goal and objectives of the strategic description for a particular project (and the choice of OO notation), the options can include:

- assignment of strategic concepts to "controller" objects;
- global and/or local constraints on object behavior;
- assignment of behavior as attributes for business objects; and/or
- incorporation as business rules.

REFERENCES

Fowler, Martin (1997). UML Distilled. Addison-Wesley Longman, Inc.

Gardner, K. (1995). KADS Object Class Syllabus.

Martin, James & J. Odell (1995). *Object-Oriented Methods: A Foundation.* Englewood Cliffs, NJ: Prentice-Hall.

Rumbaugh, J., M. Blaha, W. Premerlani, F. Eddy & W. Lorensen (1991). *Object Oriented Modeling and Design.* Englewood Cliffs, NJ: Prentice-Hall.

Unified Modeling Language (UML) 1.0 (1996). Specification, Rational Software. 1996

CHAPTER 5

Other Uses of KADS Object

INTRODUCTION

This chapter addresses other uses to which KADS Object has been applied. Human or system activities that are characterized as *knowledge intensive,* or that are perceived as complex, are generally considered good candidates for cognitive modeling. "Knowledge intensive" refers to any process or activity that requires the application of expert reasoning and problem-solving ability based on subject-area knowledge.

To date, KADS Object has been applied in four general areas:

- a knowledge acquisition and design method for knowledge-based systems (the original purpose of the Esprit KADS-I initiative);
- a cognitive pattern framework for object-oriented analysis and design for system development;
- a cognitive pattern framework for business process object modeling for the purpose of business process redesign, reengineering or process improvement;
- a cognitive pattern framework for modeling technical architecture for object-oriented systems.

There is a wealth of information on KADS pertaining to the first bullet (knowledge-based systems), available in published literature and public-domain papers from the Esprit/KADS project. Therefore it will not be addressed here. The second bullet (pattern framework for object-oriented analysis and design) is discussed in detail in chapters 2, 3, 4, and 9, and is the primary focus of this book. The application of KADS Object to technical architecture is discussed in chapter 6.

This chapter briefly introduces several other diverse uses of KADS Object:

- business process modeling;
- enterprise metamodels;
- knowledge management;
- design patterns and use cases;
- business rules;
- user requirements;
- skill set requirements;
- training development.

Each is discussed in the sections below.

BUSINESS PROCESS MODELING

KADS Object, as it has been applied in enterprise and process modeling, has provided a means for effectively modeling existing processes as well as redesigned and reengineered processes. Development of cognitive patterns often reveals subtle yet important differences in the way a task is addressed by an expert as opposed to an novice, which can facilitate immediate benefits through simple process improvement measures guided by the cognitive patterns.

The following short case example illustrates this point.

> The spare-parts division of a manufacturing company was experiencing a broad range of performance differences among their staff. Although the twenty employees of the division possessed roughly the same educational and experience skill levels, only five of the staff were considered true "experts" at determining spare-parts stocking and reorder levels. "Expert" in this case was measured in terms of maintaining adequate stock levels to handle variable manufacturing loads, while minimizing inventory and overhead costs.
>
> After several attempts at revising training and documentation materials relating to the task, there was no measurable improve-

ment in performance. Management decided to develop cognitive patterns reflecting the work of the spare-parts division staff. The purpose of this exercise was to determine if the cognitive patterns could reveal some "hidden" or embedded knowledge that the experts were applying to the task— knowledge that might be leveraged effectively to the entire division. Cognitive patterns were developed of experts for the stocking and reordering process. In parallel, patterns were developed for the nonexperts for the same process. A comparison was made between the patterns, and the differences became apparent quickly.

Although everyone in the division had access to the same information, the experts utilized certain types of information in much more effective ways. For example, experts always compared historical data on stock levels for certain parts against market forecasts. They established fairly predictable patterns of spare-parts demand at different times of year, and reordered accordingly, always maintaining optimum levels for manufacturing. The non-expert staff stocked and reordered spare parts by more of an ad hoc, seat-of-the-pants approach. They often found themselves overstocked with some parts, and backordered on other parts, never managing to maintain a good balance.

Knowledge of the problem solving employed by the experts was formalized into a new set of guidelines and policies for the spare-parts division, and resulted in a dramatic improvement in their overall performance and cost-effectiveness to the company.

This small effort resulted in immediate business value to the company, purely on the basis of process improvement and redesign, without regard to OO or software deliverables. At the same time, this company was applying the principles of knowledge management by capturing, validating and distributing knowledge and expertise to the enterprise.

The example above illustrates a simple application of *process improvement,* based on some obvious behavior modifications guided by the cognitive patterns of experts.

DEVELOPING ENTERPRISE METAMODELS

At the enterprise level, KADS Object patterns can be developed that capture all core business functions, primary inputs/outputs, and all interrelationships across the enterprise within a problem-solving, results-oriented, knowledge-using context. These enterprise metapatterns have proven very useful in early vision/strategy/planning phases—to gain a holistic view of an organization and consensus among stakeholders on where the critical areas of corporate knowledge/expertise exist, how project activities should be prioritized, and illuminating obvious candidates for process redesign. In addition, existing systems can be mapped to the cognitive enterprise metapatterns, indicating the extent to which an existing system supports one or more operations in the templates. This activity presupposes a legacy inventory has been developed, which can then be mapped to the patterns. Figure 5.1 shows a template where the percentage coverage by particular legacy systems is indicated (e.g., for the operation "compose," the legacy application referred to as "Cobra" covers the desired functionality by 50 percent; the operation "monitor" is assisted by several applications with a combined coverage of 100 percent). This allows organizations to assess their automated support for these cognitive operations and provides a basis for gap analysis. For instance, when each system to be mapped is shown as a specific color overlay on a template, it is obvious when there are redundancies (i.e., several systems supporting the same operation) and where there are gaps in coverage. The gap analysis can be as detailed as desired.

KNOWLEDGE MANAGEMENT

Patterns offer a formalized approach and notation for representing knowledge. If an organization models all of its core business and sustaining processes from this perspective, and reorganizes itself to take advantage of this "meta-knowing," then the organization begins to resemble a "knowledge organization" and can begin to reap the benefits of its knowledge assets. If, in addition to using this approach, an emphasis is placed on reusability, "knowledge reengineering" and lessons learned, then the organization begins to resemble a powerful "learning organization" by leveraging existing knowledge into new forms of knowledge.

Although the ideas of "knowledge" and "problem solving" are intriguing for their own sake, they have practical applications. The use and implementation of these ideas by organizations assists them in viewing themselves as a set of dynamic problem-solving processes rather than as a stale set of data flows and process hand-offs. Identifying the major types, sources and locations of organi-

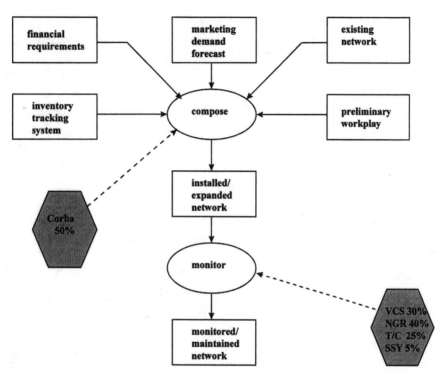

FIGURE 5.1. Gap Analysis Example

zational expertise (intellectual assets) allows for the management of these assets.

PATTERNS AND USE CASES

At some point it is useful to map design patterns to the template operations. As discussed previously, each operation can be viewed as a high-level pattern. However, we believe that mapping design patterns to the operations provides a useful context for design patterns, a kind of use guide. Eventually, a repository of design patterns can be developed for each operation and/or template that would be useful to maintain in a particular setting. For instance, in a robotics setting, the "select" operation may require design patterns that reflect "pattern matching" and "determination of degrees of freedom."

Use cases, in our experience, are often misapplied. As an example, one organization recently developed, over the course of several months, several hundred use cases at varying levels of abstraction. A couple of months were then wasted attempting to find value in the use cases that had been so painstakingly accumulated. Eventually, they had to start over again, because the lack of a common underlying structure or context meant there was no way to evaluate the relevancy of individual use cases. The application of use cases without a sense of context and recognition of the boundary conditions for a project can lead to confusion.

In our experience, the problem-solving templates provide a much needed context for use cases. Depending on the level of abstraction desired, use cases can be developed for the template or for individual operations within a template.

The list of basic steps that are involved in the application of use cases to problem-solving templates is as follows:

1. Identify the purpose of the use case.
2. Describe the actors (e.g., users) for each template (or operation).
3. Identify the preconditions.
4. Identify the primary flow of the use case, including the type of requirements the actors have regarding the view/manipulation of the template/operation. Identify events that must send notification to the actors when they occur.
5. Identify the post conditions.
6. Identify any alternative flow.

Applying the notion of a use case to the "Systematic Diagnosis" template (using the plant-problem example in chapter 4), candidates for actors would include botanists, nonprofessional nursery personnel, customers, and so forth. The primary flow would describe such items as the screen design for the entering of the complaint, and the input required from the user. If, as is usually the case, there were several templates where customer was an actor, the combined-use cases where customer was an actor could be identified and tracked.

As with patterns, use cases can be applied at all levels of abstraction, depending on the needs of the project. The boundary between analysis and design is fluid.

IDENTIFYING/DEVELOPING BUSINESS RULES

Identification of business rules is accomplished during the task of modeling of the pattern description and problem-solving template. Generally, the analyst elicits business rules on a template-by-template basis. Business rules are classified as either global or local. Often, global business rules impact one or more templates, or core processes. Global business rules can be derived from corporate policies such as "all customer inquiries shall be resolved in real time" or "new orders will not be processed for accounts with balances over 90 days past due."

Local business rules impact a more constrained area such as an operation (e.g., "all contaminated soil samples must be fumigated after testing"). This example of a local business rule could be associated with a specific operation such as "specify appropriate tests" within the context of the "Systematic Diagnostic" template.

Business rules are controls that ensure the functionality of the process. At a low level, they guide the behavior of objects in order to produce process outputs. They can also establish the conditions for beginning or completing a given process, and are used to address exceptions and to enforce performance requirements. Global business rules are usually modeled as object types themselves, whereas local business rules are constraints on specific object type behavior.

Although the subject of inferencing in object-oriented systems is a topic unto itself, it is briefly discussed in this section because inferencing rules can be considered a kind of business rule. The difference between inferencing (i.e., intelligent) rules and normal business rules is that inferencing rules chain together. Depending on the output of a given rule, that inferencing rule "fires" other rules. The path of this chaining inference cannot be easily predicted; it is difficult, if not impossible, to know which rules will fire at any point in time. Normal business rules, on the other hand, are more "stand alone," often acting as constraints on behavior; therefore they are less problematic. To date, no existing major object notation accounts for chaining rules; among the reasons for this is that chaining rules can adversely affect encapsulation. Hence, when we embed intelligence (i.e., use chaining inference rules) in object-oriented systems, we must adapt the object notation so that the chaining rules can be modeled and logically incorporated.

DEVELOPING USER REQUIREMENTS

For a variety of reasons discussed in earlier chapters, user requirements for systems development are often as elusive as the embedded knowledge of the subject-matter expert. The templates can serve as the context for eliciting general user requirements. Further development of business object models, and development of conceptual architecture can provide specific functional specifications in support of the user requirements.

In the course of iterative development of the KADS Object model, new aspects of the business process are illuminated to the subject-matter expert, and new ideas emerge relating to concepts, behaviors and their interrelationships. It has not been uncommon to hear comments such as "I didn't realize I used that information in my decision making," or "I've been performing this task for a long time, and never quite understood how it worked until now." Concepts and behaviors necessary to perform knowledge-work can be expressed very succinctly and, in turn, be used to represent complete, tested sets of user requirements.

User requirements are usually associated with operations and use cases. For instance, a "select" operation can have user requirements at a functional level (i.e., "What exactly must the "select" operation perform?"), and at the use-case level (e.g., "What actors are involved?" "What does the screen design need to incorporate?"). Examples of user requirements are described in the case study in chapter 9.

IDENTIFYING SKILL SET REQUIREMENTS

KADS Object templates can be used as a guidelines for establishing skill requirements for various tasks. This technique can be effective when used in conjunction with use-case development for the templates. The use cases identify the business roles ("actors") that apply and use the knowledge. Skill requirements as they relate to specific tasks described in the use cases can be analyzed for the purposes of business process redesign. New "knowledge worker" roles can be identified, where the skill sets required for one specific pattern might be more effectively applied across several related patterns. Also, this type of analysis can aid in development of detailed and specific skill requirements for various roles. The skill set requirements can be identified at the template level or at the template operation level.

TRAINING DEVELOPMENT

Boeing Commercial Airplane Group (Trott, 1996) has successfully developed training programs designed to speed the knowledge-transfer process by creating knowledge models of expert users based on KADS. These programs have been deployed, with measurable positive impact on the organization.

Boeing sought to shorten the nine-month learning curve for users of CAD/CAM software by teaching them the thinking process and strategies of expert users. They used KADS modeling techniques to identify, capture and analyze the thinking practices of experts.

The methodology is designed to describe explicitly how experts use certain information to solve problems, deal with uncertainty and minimize risks. Boeing has used KADS as the basis for instructional design, reference documentation and process improvements.

Traditionally, Boeing training staff use task analysis to develop course content. This is appropriate for tasks that can be directly observed and have a degree of procedure. However, task analysis has proven inadequate for tasks with heavy cognitive components, tasks where a subject-matter expert thinks a great deal prior to acting. KADS is used here to make the nonobservable thinking processes explicit.

The knowledge models used at Boeing were created by skilled analysts through structured interviews and observations of expert users over a period of three to four months. The analysts then worked with course developers to identify learning objectives and integrate the identified CAD/CAM best-thinking practices into the training curriculum. Thus far, instructional designers have used the knowledge models to:

- identify or create training examples that illustrate specific cognitive tasks;
- develop a reference book that describes the knowledge models;
- create single- or multiple-task–based training courses (in which the models define the outline and concepts on which the course will focus);
- create skill checks to test whether the student can perform the critical cognitive tasks at the desired level of proficiency;
- identify specific points in the training curricula where expert processes should be used;
- begin a dialog with the process documentation staff to integrate these expert-thinking processes into their processes and standards;
- create on-line simulations and job aids.

Boeing has married the KADS approach to training and process improvements. Their intention is not to replace the experts, but to transfer expert-thinking strategies quickly, effectively and inexpensively.

Boeing has measured the impact of this practice in three ways:

1. Estimated return on investment.

A conservative estimate of return on investment for one airplane program was 4000 percent per year, based on reductions in the lost time of new users, the decreased inefficiency of current users, fewer errors in data sets, and less demand on computing resources by inefficient data sets. That estimate also included an increase in the ease of modification of data sets.

2. Testing students' abilities to perform the new skills.

In one small field test of 70 students trained in CAD/CAM best-thinking practices and 30 untrained employees, the results were clear:

- All of the trained employees were able to construct a simple solid successfully while not even half of the untrained employees were able to do so.
- The slowest student time among trained employees was about equal to the fastest student time among the untrained employees.
- Trained employees produced almost all accurate models while untrained employees created mostly inaccurate models.
- Models produced by trained employees had fairly efficient construction, while models from untrained employees had inefficient construction.
- Most trained employees could correctly plan more complex parts, which they were able to construct in CAD/CAM, untrained employees could not.

3. Decreased time in learning changes to CAD/CAM.

As changes are made to the CAD/CAM program, training and process documents must be updated as well. They will measure whether it is possible to implement these changes faster for each major block point of the CAD/CAM software.

BUILDING CASE BASES

Boeing Commercial Airplane Group in collaboration with Inference Corporation (Trott & Leng, 1996) have done some interesting applications of KADS modeling to support the building of commercial case bases using a CBR engine. They have used the KADS methods to capture and describe the domains of interest for their case bases, as well as developing models of expertise in diagnosis and classification. They have found that the KADS PSTs can provide a very significant "jump start" on modeling troubleshooting cases that are typical of CBR case bases. Also, they documented process improvements in building case bases using KADS in the following areas:

- *Reduction in analysis time:* they were able to create a robust, medium-sized casebase (550+ cases, 100 questions, 180 actions) in only 9 weeks.
- *Consensus on logic:* the PSTs provided the SMEs with a common language from which to agree on logic and efficiency of the troubleshooting approach.
- *Improved quality:* they were able to create a casebase with virtually no logic errors, and were able to tune the performance in minutes rather than hours.

REFERENCES

Tansley & Hayball (1995). *Knowledge-Based Systems Analysis and Design: A KADS Developer's Handbook.* Englewood Cliffs, NJ: Prentice-Hall.

Trott, J. (1995). *Knowledge Modeling to Capture, Analyze and Transfer Expert Thinking.* American Society for Training and Development.

Trott, J. & Leng, B. (1996). *An Engineering Approach to Building Troubleshooting Casebases.* Boeing White Paper.

Fowler, M. (1997). *Analysis Patterns: Reusable Object Models.* Reading, MA: Addison-Wesley.

Gardner, K. (1995). *Position Paper on Knowledge Management.* CSC White Paper.

PART 3

Applied Cognitive Patterns: Best-Practice Models and Case Study

Summary

Part 3 consists of:

Chapter 6—Best Practice: Technical Architecture
Chapter 7—Best-Practice Reuse
Chapter 8—Best Practice: Testing OO Systems
Chapter 9—Case Study: A Retail Banking Example

This section provides examples of patterns developed from best practices of typical OO life-cycle activities. Each activity explores the differences between the application of cognitive patterns vs.a traditional approach, and is drawn from direct project experience. The section concludes with a case study based upon an actual project, which ties together the pattern development processes discussed throughout the book in a common thread, and includes anecdotal references to common pitfalls and areas of greatest perceived business value.

Objectives

The objectives of part 3 are:

- To provide detailed examples of KADS Object patterns, directly applied to best practice in OO development;
- To contrast the specific differences between cognitive approaches and traditional approaches as applied to OO development;
- To reinforce the concepts and techniques of cognitive patterns by applying theory to a specific case-study example.

CHAPTER 6

Best Practice: Technical Architecture

PURPOSE

This chapter has two major purposes: to illustrate the use of cognitive patterns for describing *how* to design and implement technical architecture, to define and justify the importance of technical architecture, and the use of patterns to describe it.

Technical architecture that is designed and built properly is an important asset to large organizations. Unfortunately, this value is not easily recognized. In fact, it is our contention that most organizations rarely understand or appreciate the advantages achieved by building a solidly constructed architecture. They tend to simply view technical architecture as the totality of all of the organization's automated systems.

In most organizations, the focus is on the development of applications. Such development is bottom-up and ad hoc because the organization must quickly address the information technology backlog. Following this approach without regard for the evolving "Big Picture," however, has resulted in poorly developed systems consisting of client/server islands of information.

From a software engineering perspective, improperly or nonarchitected systems are no different from the legacy systems we are reengineering today. They are proprietary, and tend to be informally designed and documented. Furthermore, they do not integrate well with other systems or fit into an overall architecture (Andrews, 1994). Despite these drawbacks, management often questions the time and money spent on the development of a technical architecture. The preference is to purchase a client/server development environment and hope to rapidly develop their way out of any predicament in which they find themselves.

To be effective, a technical architecture must exhibit a synergistic effect in which the overall system provides functions and features that individual system elements alone cannot provide. By synergy we mean "...behavior of whole systems unpredicted by the separately observed behaviors of any of the systems' separate parts or any subassembly of the systems parts" (Fuller, 1971). Furthermore, the architecture must guarantee that the entire system adapt to and display a predictable desired behavior when it becomes unstable through faults or saturation. In contrast, poorly or informally designed architectures, where attention has been primarily bestowed on the individual parts (i.e., applications) of the entire system, are characterized primarily by unpredictable behavior, resulting in crashes or corrupted queues.

As mentioned previously, the specific purpose of this chapter is to define what we mean by technical architecture, and identify the benefits of developing it by using a cognitive pattern approach. Also, we want to examine how a cognitive pattern approach differs from traditional approaches for developing technical architecture. Finally, we want to present cognitive patterns for some of the aspects of development of technical architecture.

DEFINITION

We define "technical architecture" as the conceptual, logical and physical frameworks that describe the structure, behavior and collaborations of complex system elements required to fulfill the goals of the organization. This definition implies that technical architecture is more than a collection of hardware, software and communication-enabling components; it forms the underlying infrastructure for the implementation of core business processes. Technical architecture is viewed as sets of interacting patterns (cognitive and design).

DIMENSIONS OF TECHNICAL ARCHITECTURE

In our view, there are three dimensions that can be used to describe technical architecture. They are:

1. development phases;
2. modeling approaches;
3. technical architecture components.

The relationship among the development phases, modeling approaches and technical-architecture components are shown in figure 6.1. The dimensions are described in further detail below.

Development Phase Dimension

The development phase dimension consists of information-technology (IT) vision and strategy, and the conceptual design, logical design, and physical implementation subphases. The conceptual, logical and physical design elements together represent a more traditional approach for developing software. Although these three elements are acceptable for applications, the vision and strategy component is necessary for technical architectures.

IT vision and strategy describes the long-term direction, planning goals and objectives that are aligned with corporate strategies. Business vision and strategies are used as guidelines to determine IT requirements for functionality, resilience to change and quality of service. Without synchronizing business and

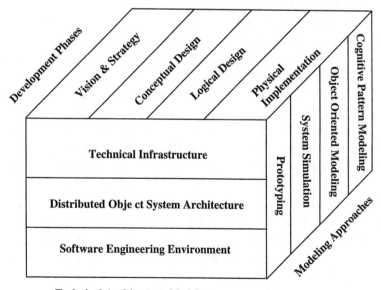

Technical Architecture Models

FIGURE 6.1. Dimensions of Technical Architecture

IT vision and strategies, business and technical functions will most likely have a negative impact on the successful implementation of distributed systems.

The conceptual design model defines the required system functionality and explains why it is required. This model also defines the system elements, such as servers, clients, an ORB, and back-end legacy systems. The model also defines the critical interfaces between these elements (Rechtin, 1991).

The logical design model formalizes the relationship between system elements and the interfaces. System objects are detailed at a level adequate for physical implementation. All collaborations are defined, with focus on form, in order to maximize cohesion and minimize coupling. The resulting model is resilient to changes requested by users and implemented by developers.

Physical implementation involves the actual construction of the architecture and its systems. This task is highly dependent on decisions made in the selection of the software engineering environment and the experience of the development staff.

Modeling Approaches

Technical architecture modeling is conducted at several levels. Pattern modeling, object-oriented modeling, simulation, and prototyping are activities important for the development of a technical architecture.

Cognitive patterns represent the highest abstraction within the modeling dimension. Core concepts of the technical architecture are identified and basic functionality is determined. KADS Object is used to obtain a cognitive view of technical architecture.

OO modeling translates the cognitive pattern view to one expressed in an object-oriented form. Categories of hardware and networking components (servers, clients, routers, printers, etc.) and capabilities are identified. The categories are mapped to classes and relevant behavior is determined. Any object notation (UML, OPEN, Martin & Odell, for example) may be used in the mapping.

System simulation allows the technical-architecture object model to be tested prior to its actual implementation. The behavior of the proposed architecture is modeled at this time. The purpose of simulation is to determine the performance and scalability attributes of the design prior to actual hardware and development tool purchases.

Prototyping is used for two purposes. The first is to drive out additional requirements not initially identified or understood in the cognitive models of the technical architecture. The second purpose is to validate existing requirements.

Technical-Architecture Components Dimension

Technical infrastructure defines the structure of the system in the specific areas of hardware, system software, and communications networks. At this level, transaction volumes/sizes are modeled to determine the computer hardware, network, and system software (e.g., database) requirements. In an object-oriented environment, these requirements and the associations between business objects and enterprise locations are used to design the infrastructure down to the configurable component level. Since system management and support tools are dependent on the technical infrastructure, their requirements are determined as part of the technical infrastructure development activities.

System architecture defines the "overall structure of a system, including its partitioning into subsystems and their allocation to tasks and processors" (Rumbaugh, 1991). In an OO environment, system architecture deals with the structural and behavioral development of active and passive objects within an application as realized through the technical infrastructure. Careful attention must be paid to object service levels, affinities between objects and the protocols used to communicate between objects (synchronous, asynchronous, etc.). For example, the system architecture determines which objects collaborate using a client/server communications model versus a group multicast communications model.

The software-engineering environment defines the tools and techniques for creating and maintaining elements in support of the system architecture. Object-oriented software-engineering environments vary in their offerings of tools, from complete application development and deployment environments such as **Førté, Neuron Data** and **NextStep**, to those used for integrating objects and relational databases, such as **Persistence**. The choices are very broad and have impacts on other architectural objectives, such as security and performance.

BUSINESS CASE FOR TECHNICAL ARCHITECTURE

We believe that business processes are enabled by the design and implementation characteristics of the technical architecture. Granted, this is an entirely technocentric point of view. Our contention, however, is that technology functions at times as an impetus for new business processes, not necessarily the other way around. The strategic advantage in developing a technical architecture, therefore, is that it permits the creation, extension and enhancement of new or existing business capabilities. Implicit in this outlook is that technology and process are closely coupled. Further, a properly designed architecture is an unbounded construct, in the sense that changes to the business model can be reflected in the architecture.

The role of the information-technology organization has changed dramatically in the past ten years with the advent of powerful development tools and the move toward decentralized computing. Business units within many organizations, for example, have acquired their own IT resources and currently develop custom (legacy) applications without consideration of an approach that leverages the value of an overall technical architecture. In addition, the business environment has become extremely dynamic. The business process reengineering movement and approaches to continuous improvement are responses to the constant change found in today's business environment (Hammer & Champy, 1993). IT has had to adapt accordingly.

A central theme in business system development is the requirement for modular and configurable business processes. This requirement is mirrored in the so-called plug-and-play architectures that provide suitable flexibility so that organizations are responsive to both customers and competition. Responsiveness to customers requires technologies that enable the provisioning of superior services. Technologies must permit the modification of these services as customer's needs change.

Responsiveness to competition requires that the organization be able to rapidly reconfigure itself and its systems in order to adapt to competitors' changes and implementations of key market differentiators. Today IT is an essential enabler with businesses striving to take advantage of technology push strategies to remain competitive.

The structure and behavior of the applications needed to support business drivers are dramatically different from those implemented on host-centric systems, which served the enterprises' accounting functions faithfully for many years. The move from host-centric, vendor-driven environments to heterogeneous, distributed, multi-vendor environments using powerful software development tools has provided a tremendous amount of flexibility in how systems are developed.

Flexibility is a double-edged sword, however, and it carries a hidden price. Flexibility adds complexity that was previously factored out or managed by the vendor. The increase in complexity of design, implementation and maintenance is caused by the fundamental characteristics of plug-and-play distributed systems (Coulouris et al., 1994). These characteristics are:

- Resource sharing—provides system users with uniform reference and access to hardware, communication and software objects in a distributed scheme;

- Openness—determines how extensible a particular system is with respect to hardware, software and communications and how easily attainable through object interface specifications; often associated with adherence to established or de facto standards;
- Concurrency—ability of the system to provide service to multiple clients, providing users with a single system image and an established quality of service while maintaining system integrity;
- Scalability—ability to accept new resources to meet the demands of increased load;
- Fault Tolerance—insures that mission-critical services are correctly performed and completed; and
- Transparency—determines to what extent the underlying network, protocols, hardware and system software is hidden from the user; provides users with a seamless single-system view of what may be a complex, distributed, heterogeneous environment.

These characteristics impact the design of the entire system and require balanced decisions around architecture and engineering to meet the goals of the enterprise. A modular and configurable technical architecture is required to effectively manage the complexity of large-scale systems in order to guarantee functionality, provide resilience to change and insure quality of service.

Guaranteed functionality means that a system must do what it is intended to do. The system must provide an acceptable level of performance, reliability, availability, scalability, consistency and security. These components are often at odds, necessitating trade-off analyses when developing the technical architecture. For instance, there are a variety of schemes for securing a system with some of the more thorough methods having a negative impact on performance. Balancing these components to meet business requirements is an architectural task that results in formalized security and performance policies that management uses to guide development.

Resilience to change is an attribute of the architecture that is expressed in a modular design. Modularity permits the organization to more easily maintain the existing architectural structure or add new technology to it. If changes are required, they can be made without interrupting the underlying functionality. Resilience to change means that the design and implementation of the architecture is focused on form, maximum cohesiveness and minimum coupling.

Quality of service is closely tied to guaranteed functionality. Performance, reliability, availability and security are important considerations here as well.

Each of these elements must be well understood and articulated in the design. For example, if a system must be available twenty-four hours every day, it may be necessary to create redundant paths so as to insure failover.

TECHNICAL ARCHITECTURE: TRADITIONAL VS. COGNITIVE APPROACH

As has been illustrated above, complexity is the hallmark of technical-architecture structure and development. During the 1970s and 1980s, complexity was rarely an issue, as most software-engineering efforts were much smaller than they are today. Mainframes were the standard hardware platform and discussions around such topics as "distributed services" were mostly theoretical. Thus, traditional approaches to the development of technical architecture are largely inadequate for the kinds of systems needed today. Today there are many different diagrams that are used to model architecture, with little coherence evident between them.

One alternative is to examine technical architecture from a cognitive pattern point of view. That is, a cognitive pattern approach clarifies what kinds of information are pertinent to the development of a technical architecture, and presents a uniformed consistent view of the functions of a technical architecture. The cognitive pattern approach provides a problem solving view that can serve as a coherent picture of the behavior of a technical architecture.

Differences between traditional approaches for developing technical architecture compared with the KADS approach are summarized in table 6.1.

OTHER CONSIDERATIONS

Technical infrastructure, system architecture and the software-engineering environment are the three principle components of technical architecture. Each are influenced and developed during the conceptual and logical design, with IT vision and strategy guiding the development effort. The development and design is accomplished using an iterative/incremental approach and is not based on the "waterfall" life cycle.

To develop an approach for technical architecture, it is important to understand the nature of each technical-architecture development phase. Technical-architecture development is part art and part science. As an art form, technical architecture is a creative, nonlinear cognitive task that deals primarily with concepts. At the conceptual level, the architect strives to maintain a fit and balance with what is feasible in reality (that is, looking toward implementation). At this

TABLE 6.1. Traditional Approaches vs. KADS

Traditional Approach	KADS Approach
Focus on the "how" of technical architecture development; emphasis on "cans and wires"	Focus on the "what" of technical architecture development; emphasis on patterns
Relationship between technical architecture development phases, architectural components, and modeling approachesnot clearly articulated	Relationship between technical architecture development phases, architectural models, and modeling approaches clearly articulated
Business objectives which influence technical architecture not always apparent	Business objectives, expressed in patterns, can be directly linked to patterns in the architecture, by phase and by model
No clear understanding of the influence of technical architecture on business objectives	Greater comprehension of the influence of technical architecture on the creation, extension, and enhancement of new or existing business capabilities
The relationship between technical architecture and the non functional requirements such as security, reliability and availability is not always clear	Greater understanding of the relationship between the technical architecture and nonfunctional requirements because of the ability to indicate the pattern relationships , e.g., the relationship between the "security pattern(s)" and the patterns associated with "distributed object system architecture".

conceptual level the focus is on tasks (processes) that must be performed by the proposed system. The scientific aspect of technical architecture is a logical and analytical linear task that deals with well-defined problems and is more applicable to the logical model. At this level the focus is on system engineering or the form of the system. The linear and nonlinear aspects do not take place in isolation, but one aspect is predominant in each task.

Because of the difference between linear and non-linear modeling, important information is often lost between the conceptual level and the logical level. Our approach is to base the modeling that is performed at both levels on the notion of an architectural framework composed of cognitive patterns and design patterns, which are then mapped to an object notation. What is an architectural framework and what are design patterns? According to Coplien and Schmidt:

"Architectural frameworks express a fundamental paradigm for structuring software systems. They provide a set of pre-defined subsystems as well as rules and guidelines for organizing the relationships between them" (1995).

These frameworks provide a context to describe the overall system architecture discussed previously. And frameworks are composed of cognitive patterns and design patterns.

Architectural design Patterns describe a basic scheme for structuring subsystems and components of system architectures, as well as the relationship between them. It identifies names and abstracts a common design principle by describing its different parts and their collaboration and responsibility" (Coplien & Schmidt, 1995).

The architect utilizes a repository of architectural frameworks and patterns and builds a conceptual model to drive selection of implementation components and logical design. The components, along with their strengths and weaknesses, are reviewed with the client and a selection is made based on "fit, balance, and compromise" (Rechtin, 1991). The conceptual models are mapped to static and dynamic object models that reflect the logical model for validation using a CASE tool (preferably capable of animation [e.g., LiveModel]).

Modeling the technical architecture as a set of collaborative objects based on the frameworks and patterns helps the technical architect meet the goal of seamless integration between the conceptual and logical domains to maintain conceptual integrity and preservation of architecture in the system.

The logical design is validated and verified using static and dynamic testing, performance modeling, reliability testing, and quality-assurance testing. Inconsistencies or defects found at this point are still inexpensive to fix and modifications can be made to the models with minor impact. The logical model is validated with a focus on form, maximum cohesiveness, and minimal coupling, to ensure resilience to change. Simulations or prototypes may be developed to test the behavior of the proposed design without actually having to implement the system. Once validated, the object designers drive the logical design down to the level where either (1) system builders can create the implementation from the tested models, or (2) the implementation can be generated by a CASE tool capable of code generation.

BEST-PRACTICE PATTERN: TECHNICAL ARCHITECTURE

The following section presents the application of cognitive patterns to the *development* of a technical architecture.

Cognitive Technical-Architecture Patterns

The high level of "Technical-Architecture Development Pattern" is composed of the patterns required to develop the following three components:

1. Distributed-Object–System Architecture;
2. Technical Infrastructure;
3. Software-Engineering Environment.

Each of these components is composed of the common development phase deliverables described previously in Figure 6.1. The following templates *may* be executed top-down, bottom-up, sequential or in parallel, depending on the context and complexity of the problem domain. A strategy must be developed for each specific project that orchestrates the execution of these patterns in order to develop a robust technical architecture.

The following discussion illustrates the high level technical-architecture development pattern diagram, its associated pattern description, its concept description and selected drill down into its operations.

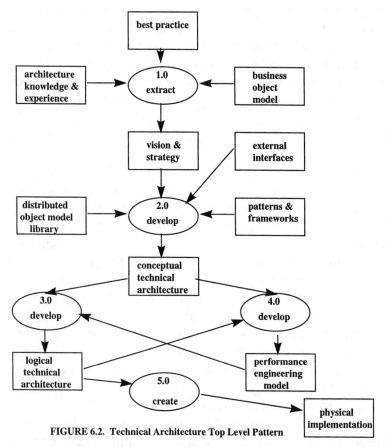

FIGURE 6.2. Technical Architecture Top Level Pattern

FIGURE 6.2. Technical-Architecture Development Pattern

TECHNICAL-ARCHITECTURE DEVELOPMENT PATTERN

Pattern Description

The high level pattern provided in figure 6.2 represents an organizational structure for developing a technical architecture. It is a very high level pattern and thus cannot be equated with any of the KADS library templates. The diagram is composed of five operations, some of which are shadowed to indicate that they will be presented as subpatterns later in greater detail. Each operation in the high-level KADS pattern is described in the following pattern description, which has been modified to include the rationale for completing each operation/subpattern.

1.0 *Extract* the vision and strategy of the system that is being architected. It is imperative that the system architect understand the business and technical vision of the subject-matter experts in the organization. A strategy for delivering the solution is developed based on this vision.

Often the architectural development runs into roadblocks when the architect and/or the stakeholders do not have a clear vision of the system goals, scope and ultimately the solution. Once the vision is understood, a strategy to fulfill that vision is communicated to the stakeholders for buy-in. Unless the architect can get the stakeholders "in the tent" with a common vision of the solution, the architectural-development program is most certainly doomed to fail.

In formulating the vision and strategy for the program, the architect relies on his architectural knowledge and experience as well as industry best practices. These concepts play a crucial role in the development of the vision and strategy because they provide a reality check (Rechtin, 1991) on whether the vision is deliverable. The information-technology industry is very familiar with stories of failed projects that were the result of a great vision but poor implementation. Many of these failures were due to unrealistic expectations on the technology as well as poor delivery, but in many cases the organization was too immature to survive the technology transfusion proposed by the architecture. For this reason, it is important to consider the process maturity of the organization that will be the ultimate user of the architecture. If the organization's process management is ad hoc or chaotic, there is likely to be too much risk associated with introducing advanced technology into the organization.

At the end of this operation, a document is developed that captures the vision and strategy for architectural development for the components technical infrastructure, the distributed-object system, and the software-engineering environment.

2.0 ***Develop*** the conceptual technical architecture. This operation entails the identification and partitioning of the core system tasks and the development of the conceptual models of the infrastructure, distributed objects, and development environment. This operation is expanded upon later in the chapter.

3.0 ***Develop*** the logical technical architecture. This operation involves the system engineering and detailed design of system. Whereas the architect partitioned the system into a loose confederation of well-defined collaborating tasks, the system engineer's role is to define the system interfaces and rules for collaboration. The system designers then detail the system out to a level where builders can implement the solution. This operation is describe more fully in a subsequent portion of this chapter.

4.0 ***Develop*** the performance engineering model. This operation entails the creation of a performance engineering model to ensure that the system will provide the levels of service envisioned by the user. For instance, the Network Model is created and is simulated to determine if the proposed architecture has enough bandwidth to service the system load. The performance engineering model is used as input to the logical design in an iterative fashion. A detailed description of this operation is found later in the chapter.

5.0 ***Create*** a physical implementation. This operation entails building the infrastructure, distributed-object system, and software engineering environment. All or parts of this activity will require highly skilled craftsmen who are well versed in the various domains, such as networks or ORBs. Once this process is completed, a physical implementation of the architecture is realized and collaborating objects can be configured to build the GUI implementations using the software-engineering environment and user-interface architecture. This effort may range from I-CASE generation of the application to Visual C++ interfacing to an ORB through the architecture.

Concept Description (with examples)

Presented below is a concept description for each of the concepts represented in figure 6.2, and which has been modified to show possible sources/format and examples.

CONCEPT NAME	DEFINITION	POSSIBLE SOURCES AND FORMAT	EXAMPLE
Best Practices	A composite view of what is considered by experts to be the best approach to solving a specific set of tasks.	Documents, published standards	"Based on a study of 50 IT organizations, technical-architecture development covers at least 4 distinct development phases with specific deliverables for each..."
Architecture Knowledge & Experience	Heuristic, embedded knowledge about technical architecture, which is acquired through experience.	Anecdotal knowledge, not typically documented.	"Our earlier attempt at technical architecture was not entirely successful because we neglected to confirm the vision and strategy with the executive committee. That oversight had significant impact on our ability to..."
Business Object Model	A set of diagrams and definitions showing the primary relationships and associated behaviors of business concepts.	Diagrams, definitions & data types, often modeled within an OO case tool.	"Our model contains a 'customer' class, which has 3 subtypes ('individual,' 'small business' and 'large business') and is related to 2 other classes: 'account' and 'product' in the following ways..."

CONCEPT NAME	DEFINITION	POSSIBLE SOURCES AND FORMAT	EXAMPLE
Vision & Strategy	The vision states the business goals, objectives and scope of the system being architected. The strategy is the tactical plan of how to achieve the vision.	Descriptive documentation, including strategic plan, architectural plans, etc.	"Our vision is to have leading market share in the North American auto-rental market by June 1998. Our strategy is to implement an intranet with intelligent agents to facilitate optimized inventory distribution."
Patterns & Frameworks	Any reusable architecture that experience has shown to solve a common problem in a specific context.	Reusable diagrammatic and code templates.	"This customer-care application bears a striking similarity to two other projects we completed last year. There appears to be a common thread between this conceptual design approach and the design approaches from the other projects . . ."
External Interface Descriptions	Interface description to systems outside the implemented architecture. A detailed and complete external interface description is essential to building seamless object wrappers.	A logical and physical description of the protocols used to communicate with systems outside of the implemented architecture.	The Customer Order Fulfillment system (COF) is a real-time system that exposes a TCP-IP socket interface at port x. The following event trace depicts the logical protocol for sending an order to the COF system.

CONCEPT NAME	DEFINITION	POSSIBLE SOURCES AND FORMAT	EXAMPLE
Distributed-Object Model Library	An interface library that seamlessly provides access to objects distributed thoughout the system environment.	A set of models and APIs that provide enough information to enable client applications to collaborate with objects represented in the library.	An object model segment depicting the class associations and relationships of the key objects in a material-distribution network. An event schema depicting the protocol for transshipping between nodes in the network. Pre- and post-conditions that are expected by the model to maintain the integrity of a transshipment transaction.
Conceptual Technical Architecture	A conceptual, or "unconstrained," framework of the technical architecture, which is an aggregation of conceptual distributed object model, conceptual infrastructure, and conceptual development environment.	A set of model-based diagrams, maintained at high level (conceptual) and easy to understand	A diagram depicting (graphically) major architectural components and their relationships, such as clusters of client work stations connected to middle-tier servers, which in turn connect to back-end mainframe systems and databases via routers and gateways.

CONCEPT NAME	DEFINITION	POSSIBLE SOURCES AND FORMAT	EXAMPLE
Logical Technical Architecture	A finer-grained "constrained" architecture that has been engineered to work within a finite set of interface styles, protocols and standards. Architectural components at the logical detail level are selected for prototyping and performance engineering, culminating in a detailed design specification.	Detailed, technical design documents including diagrams, technical specifications, interface definitions, performance engineering and simulation benchmarks.	Design specifications that drive the major components of the conceptual technical architecture to sufficiently fine-grained detail to implement.
Performance Engineering Model	A performance engineering model is a simulated implementation of the target production environment, designed to validate the technical-architecture design and make any adjustments to optimally achieve business and performance goals.	The actual performance results (documentation) of running business objects in a simulated environment, including architected messaging protocols, transaction volumes and other environmental conditions.	"Initial results of our simulated model indicate that the recommended distributed-object architecture based on an ORB and thin client approach will easily accommodate your projected transaction volumes and response times through the year 2005. It should be noted, however, that one ORB vendor clearly outperformed the other three in the following areas..."

CONCEPT NAME	DEFINITION	POSSIBLE SOURCES AND FORMAT	EXAMPLE
Physical Implementation	Creating the physical environment to enable realization of the technical architecture. This includes building the infrastructure, distributed-object system and software-engineering environment.	Physical manifestations of all architectural components (servers, ethernet cable, routers, databases, software development tools, etc.)	"The development team has been provided with a room with a Sparc 20 and 4 NT workstations connected to the network backbone. The Sparc is partitioned to include a subset of test Oracle data from our production system, and all development work stations are workgroup–enabled with version 4.0 Elements Environment under version control. The team has access to the mainframe for performance testing during off peak-hours . . ."

The nested subpatterns 2.0 (Develop Conceptual Technical Architecture), 3.0 (Develop Logical Technical Architecture) and 4.0 (Develop Performance Engineering Model) from the metapattern are shown, respectively, below in figure 6.3, figure 6.4 and figure 6.5, followed by their pattern descriptions.

Sub Pattern 2.0 (Develop Conceptual Technical Architecture): Pattern Description

2.1 *Identify* core system tasks. This operation entails the identity of the core tasks of the proposed system in each of the areas in order to meet the functional requirements of the business object model. The architect partitions

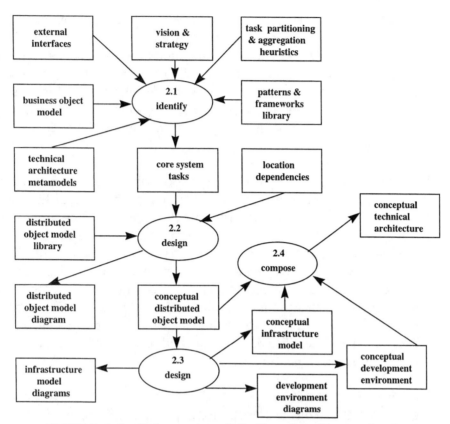

FIGURE 6.3. Subprocess 2.0: Develop Conceptual Technical Architecture

and aggregates (Rechtin, 1991) the tasks and subtasks in an effort to model component concepts and their fundamental relationships and behaviors. This is one of the most difficult aspects of system architecting due to what has been historically called the "bootstrap problem". In complex systems, the bootstrap problem is understood as not knowing where to start in discovering the core tasks and concepts. To help overcome the bootstrap problem, the architect uses heuristics (rules of thumb) and documented patterns and frameworks (Coplien & Schmidt, 1995). Technical architecture metamodels such as the CORBA reference model also help in the partitioning of the system into component parts.

Upon completion of this activity, a set of KADS Object models of the core system tasks are developed at a high level. The deliverable consists of high-level functional models, concept hierarchies, and concept definitions.

2.2 *Design* "conceptual distributed-object model." This operation involves the identification of the appropriate architectural styles from a distributed-object model library, taking into consideration the location dependencies of the system. For instance, a company may have acquired a division across the country that is the only division with specialized asynchronous data feeds requiring an agent architectural style that communicates with a daemon monitoring the feed. It is important to identify the style, as it will require specialized infrastructure support at that location.

Furthermore, it is important to develop a distributed-object model before the infrastructure and software-engineering environment, in order to maintain a higher level of abstraction for problem solving. Since a purpose of the architecture is to manage system complexity, it is imperative that overall architecture be understood. Once the structure and fundamental behavior of the system is determined, the system engineers, designers and architect can define components of the system and engineer those component to ensure that the architectural vision is complete. The output of this activity is the distributed-object model, which implements the business object model and identifies the structure and behavior of high-level system concepts to support that model.

2.3 *Design* conceptual infrastructure model and software-engineering environment model. Based on the input from the distributed-object model, the core tasks for each model are identified and executed in a manner similar to Process 2.1. For instance, the "vision' of the software engineering environment may have a task: "leverage reuse at the analysis and design level." In order to implement this task, a repository and intelligent browser may be required. The repository would impact the infrastructure model by affecting the ability of the network to work with the repository as well as with disk storage and server processing requirements.

Some iteration over the requirements and architectural styles is required in order to make the components orthogonal (possibly regrouping them) and to minimize coupling and maximize coherence.

In order to better communicate the solution and maintain conceptual integrity of the architecture, model diagrams are often created. Schematic diagrams are less understandable and tend to alienate SMEs and stakeholders of the architecture. It is important, therefore, that stakeholder-friendly diagrams be created, distributed, *and* maintained.

2.4 *Compose* the "conceptual technical architecture." This process involves reviewing the models and diagrams with the stakeholders, making the necessary revisions, and obtaining sign-off before proceeding. The models are then placed under change control to safeguard their content. With respect to project management, the completion of this activity is a major milestone.

Sub Pattern 3.0 (Develop Logical Technical Architecture): Pattern Description

This operation entails the identification and specification of the interfaces between the components of the architecture defined in the conceptual model by the system

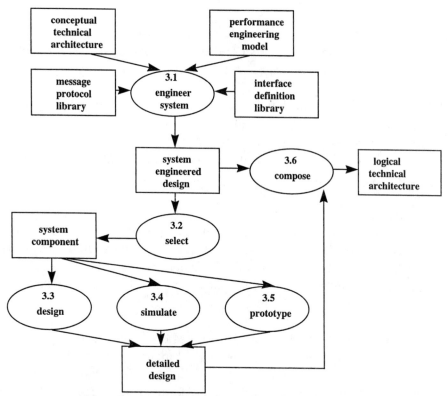

FIGURE 6.4. Subprocess 3.0: Develop Logical Technical Architecture

engineers. Each component is designed to a level of detail suitable for creation of the performance engineering model. The result of this task is a detailed specification of the interfaces and components to a level suitable for implementation.

3.1 *Engineer System* and create a "system-engineered design." This process requires the development of a detailed analysis, specification and design of the component interfaces. The system engineer, working with a finite set of interface styles, protocols and standards, specifies the allowable system interfaces to be used in the implementation of the system. In a distributed-object system, this will include a messaging strategy and message-stream definition (such as semantic data streams), using standard protocols to meet overall performance requirements. This is not a trivial task and requires considerable systems experience and more manpower than the conceptual architecture task.

3.2 *Select* the system component for design. Based on dependencies determined by the system architect and project manager, a system component is chosen for detailed design.

3.3 *Design* the detailed design. Each component of the conceptual architecture is decomposed in greater detail to a level where a solution can be synthesized. Based on the principles and standards of the architecture and engineering efforts, designers create detailed designs that can be implemented by the system builders.

3.4 *Simulate* the detailed design. Simulation is a tool that should be in every designer's toolkit. It is important that the designer be able to animate/simulate their designs to ensure that they meet the system requirements. Ideally the designers work in a distributed simulation environment where they share simulation sets of targeted system loads and capacities with the performance-engineering role.

3.5 *Prototype* the detailed design. Sometimes the only way to truly understand the requirements and behavior of a component is to actually build a scaled-down version of the implementation. This activity is akin to breadboarding in digital design and is an important tool for the system designer. Prototyping activities must be well defined and then viewed for what they are: an incomplete, quick-and-dirty reality check. Certainly parts of the prototype may be scaled, reengineered to standards and integrated into the overall design. It is important that prototypes not move directly into production.

3.6 ***Compose*** the "logical technical architecture." This task requires reviewing the designs with the system engineer and architect to insure that they comply with the system standards and do not violate conceptual integrity constraints. The designs are then placed under change control to safeguard their content. With respect to project management, the completion of this activity is a major milestone.

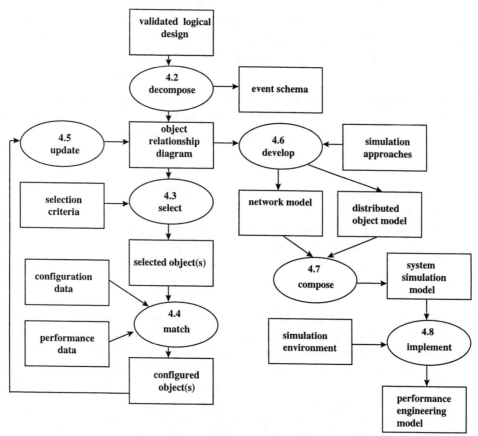

**FIGURE 6.5. Subprocess 4.0: Develop
Performance-Engineering Model**

Sub Process 4.0 (Develop Performance Engineering Model): Pattern Description

The development of a performance-engineering model allows the architect and systems engineer to estimate the performance of a technical architecture. Models are representations of actual systems. They are constructed in those instances where the real systems are too complex to understand or the costs to build them prove excessive. The advantage of modeling a system such as an architecture is to reduce the risk of its implementation by predicting with a high degree of assurance how well a particular configuration will work. Modeling involves simulation whereby the behavior of the system is imitated using particular mathematical or logical relationships. By definition, the model is inferior to a real system in that the functionality that is to be simulated is incomplete. However, this constraint makes modeling a useful and feasible activity. The goal of modeling an architecture is to produce one that captures relevant functionality and yet is parsimonious enough to be examined in a reasonable amount of time.

4.1 *Decompose* the "logical technical architecture." This process breaks the elements of the logical technical architecture into a validated logical model by further refining the technical-architecture components. The architecture model is checked for completeness and accuracy.

4.2 *Decompose* the "validated logical model." The validated logical model is decomposed further into object diagrams. These components provide the architect and system engineer with a view of the structural and behavioral aspects of the overall object model. The object model is a representation of the logical technical architecture in the form of object classes and their relationships.

4.3 *Select* a collaborating set of objects. The selected objects are chosen by some criteria that is of interest to the architect or systems engineer. The criteria may include objects that are affected or are thought to be affected by bandwidth, CPU, volume, or some other characteristic of interest.

4.4 *Match* the selected objects. The selected objects are matched to corresponding configuration and performance data. The configuration data may include criteria about a particular kind of server or bandwidth limitations of the network. The performance data may represent desired behavioral attributes such as arrival rates of transactions. The output of this process is a set of configured objects.

4.5 *Update* the "static object diagram." The static object diagram is updated based on the set of configured objects. This is an iterative process, which may be repeated until the performance engineer, system engineer and architect are satisfied with the correctness of the object model.

4.6 *Develop* a network model and a distributed-object model. The network and distributed-object models are developed based on the object model and a simulation approach. The simulation may include the development of approaches for modeling queuing limitations, timing constraints and messaging. Each of these is challenging and may require specialized knowledge or experience with the construction of stochastic and deterministic models.

4.7 *Compose* a System-Simulation Model. Using the network and distributed-object models, compose a system-simulation model. This process brings together the proposed network components as well as the proposed object components.

4.8 *Implement* the performance-engineering model. Based on a system-simulation model and a simulation environment, the performance-engineering model is built and exercised. The performance data generated by the model is used to refine the logical technical architecture.

SUMMARY

Today's dynamic business environment has placed complex demands on the use of information technology. Systems must be reliable and maintainable. They must meet specific performance levels and be usable. Furthermore, systems need to be resilient to change, despite the ever-changing structure of competitive enterprises. A well-developed and understood technical architecture allows organizations to achieve business goals and objectives by maximizing the utility of information and using emerging technologies. The use of patterns at all levels of abstraction assists the architects in managing complexity and provides an easy to understand notation for all participants. KADS patterns have been used to illustrate their use in modeling *how* to design technical architecture.

REFERENCES

Andrews, T. (1994). " 'Thick' Technical Infrastructure Enables Business Change," CSC Presentation.

Coplien, J.O. & D.C. Schmidt, eds. (1995). *Pattern Languages of Program Design*. Reading, MA: Addison-Wesley.

Coulouris, G., et al. (1994). *Distributed Systems: Concepts and Design*. Reading, MA: Addison-Wesley.

Fuller, R.B. (1971). *Operating Manual For Spaceship Earth*. NY: E.P. Dutton.

Hammer, M. & J. Champy (1993). *Reengineering the Corporation*. NY: Harpers Business.

Rechtin, E. (1991). *Systems Architecting: Creating and Building Complex Systems*. Englewood Cliffs, NJ: Prentice-Hall.

Rumbaugh, J. (1991). *Object-Oriented Modeling and Design*. Englewood Cliffs, NJ: Prentice-Hall.

Shaw, M. & D. Garlan (1996). *Software Architecture: Perspectives on an Emerging Discipline*. Englewood Cliffs, NJ: Prentice-Hall.

CHAPTER 7

Best-Practice Reuse

PURPOSE

The purpose of this chapter is to present our approach to the reuse of both patterns and object models. The objective of reuse, as it relates to OO development, is to enable the most often touted, yet seldom achieved, benefit of the technology: rapid, economical component-based software assembly. The impediments to successful reuse can generally be traced to cultural rather than technological origins, as will be discussed in this chapter. Patterns, such as those developed in KADS Object, hold great promise for reuse and distribution across an enterprise. We view distributed-knowledge models as the key to successful knowledge-management practices—the ability to capture, store, query and distribute knowledge to the enterprise. The issues facing object reuse and reuse of patterns are quite similar, as might be expected. This chapter discusses some of the central issues and approaches around effective reuse of patterns, specifically as it relates to object orientation. Patterns are used to illustrate *how* best to achieve reuse in an organization.

DEFINITION

The definition of reuse can be found by answering the question, "What is reuse?" or more specifically, "What is reusable?" All too often, this question is answered by looking at the fine-grained deliverables at the end of the development lifecycle—namely implemented class libraries. Planning for object reuse early, during the planning and modeling stages of business development, is critical for realizing economies of scale with courser grained design concepts. Developing patterns of the approach for reuse is one way to ensure that the development process will provide every opportunity, incentive and benefit to reuse common design elements. This is especially true for large and complex applications. Thus, the question of "what is reusable?" should not be limited to physical implementations of objects. Reuse of higher-level abstractions, such as best-practice models and design artifacts created early in the development life cycle, can offer immediate business value. KADS Object patterns, by nature, are designed for effective reuse.

LEVELS OF ABSTRACTION AND REUSE

Patterns, as well as object models, can be developed at any level of abstraction. Therefore reuse of these models can be realized along a continuum, from course to fine granularity as illustrated in figure 7.1.

Different kinds of business knowledge along this continuum form opportunities for knowledge modeling, and in turn for object reuse. Reuse that occurs at the course-grained end of the continuum achieves wider impact and potentially greater leverage to the enterprise.

In order to effectively reuse business concepts, they must be modeled using

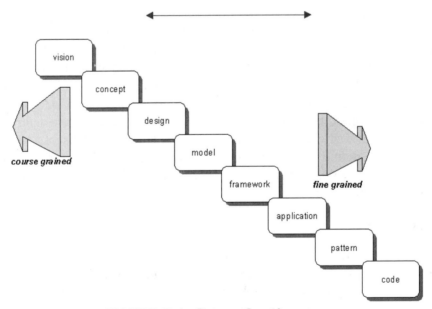

FIGURE 7.1. Reuse Continuum

a formalized approach and notation such as the KADS Object patterns, capturing the essential business information, processes, concepts, rules and assumptions upon which process and system implementations may be based. Reuse of patterns prior to implementation design not only saves resources, it can also leverage the use of "best practices" as reflected in the models.

Unfortunately, the usual approach to reuse has been to wait until an object has been "implemented" (e.g., captured in system application code), and then to think about its reuse. Objects at this end of the continuum are generally so specific as to be limited in reapplication. Addressing reuse only at the *application and code* levels tends to limit reuse to its smallest possible scope.

BUSINESS CASE FOR A PATTERN APPROACH TO REUSE

Greater economies of scale are realized by planning for effective reuse at higher levels of abstraction, and ensuring preservation of architecture throughout all reusable concept, design and implementation elements. Patterns are one of the few approaches that achieves preservation of architecture, and thus enabling effective reuse. Parallels may be drawn between deliverables (reuse candidates) in the OO development life cycle, and their corresponding level of abstraction. Table 7.1 shows the major activities of the OO development lifecycle, along with corresponding reuse candidates for each activity. Reuse candidates, in most cases, are nothing more than standard deliverables that are properly archived and retrievable for reuse.

TABLE 7.1. Life-Cycle Reuse Candidates

Life-Cycle Activities	Reuse Candidates
Strategic Business Planning, Domain Modeling	Strategic plans, business metamodels, business concepts, program/project structures, methodologies
Business Process Analysis and Design, Object Modeling	Master business cycle models, industry business metamodels, industry 'best practice' domain models, process models, object models
Application Object Modeling, OO Analysis and Design	Application class libraries, application frameworks, patterns, use cases, scripts (workflow, test)
OO Application Implementation	Implementation class libraries, components, objects, methods, code
OO Technical Architecture	Technical architecture, technical models/drawings, infrastructure documentation, patterns

KADS patterns can be used effectively for each lifecycle activity in Table 7.1 to model the activity and capture it in standard format for reuse. For example, the technical architecture and infrastructure can be modeled using KADS and design patterns, thereby abstracting it for reuse, as discussed in chapter 6. Creating an abstract cognitive pattern model that reuses concepts from high-level strategy through technical architecture supports the principle of preservation of architecture by leveraging the reuse of lower-level objects that are "compiled" in or implied by the abstract models.

When all lifecycle activities are modeled, not only is the entire OO-development process more consistent and coherent, but the design artifacts of all layers are standardized and can be offered as reusable components.

OBJECT-MODEL REUSE ENVIRONMENTS AND REPOSITORIES

The key to reusing object models is making them available and accessible to the user community, though an environment such as an object repository, object library, or object-enabled network environments. Creating environments for persistent object-model reuse offers many alternatives. However, none of the choices today could be considered entirely satisfactory. In an ideal world, reusable objects would be accessible from interpretable distributed repositories using concept browsers with open, extensible search functions. Today's commercial object repositories are moving in this direction (by using common underlying ODB systems, and common IDL specifications such as CORBA 2.0 and OLE). However, the widespread use of true interoperable OO environments is not yet a reality, both from a cultural and technological perspective.

When evaluating CASE tools, Object Databases, and other persistent object stores, it is important to ask questions regarding facilitation of reuse (i.e., consistency checking). Our experience has shown that there are variations from tool to tool in terms of their ability to enable work-group consistency and reuse.

PATTERN REPOSITORIES

Ideally, repositories for patterns will work the same way as for objects: widely distributed and accessible across heterogeneous environments. Distributed-knowledge repositories will also facilitate the ability to secure and manage knowledge assets. Today, however, we are limited to two basic strategies.

The first strategy is to leverage the persistent storage provided by tools that specifically support KADS development, such as the CommonKADS workbench, and OpenKADS (Groupe Bull). These tools were designed to support storage, retrieval, cross-referencing and manipulation of the KADS patterns. The downside to some of these tools is that they generate proprietary formats, are limited to unit-based platforms only, and tend to be rather costly.

The second strategy involves using common off-the-shelf drawing tools and databases, and creating pointers to the models from a repository, or storing models as "blobs" within an object database product (ODB), with a built-in browsing capability. We have found this strategy to be more than adequate for projects we have undertaken. The repository for patterns should include:

- a description of the function of the pattern;
- the model use across industry/function/application, etc.;
- file/tool/location pointers;
- format, tool (and version) used;
- version tracking, and authoring information;
- status of testing and QA information.
- ability to nest design patterns within higher level KADS patterns

Even with this simple reuse-repository strategy, many issues remain unresolved: security/authorization regarding patterns and sets of patterns; searching for functionality (limited to manually inserted keys); synchronization of access/update; versioning and QA assurance; status reporting of pattern use; and management of pattern life cycle to name but a few.

For more information on these subjects and on repository issues consult the references cited at the end of this chapter.

BEST-PRACTICE PATTERN: REUSE

The scope of reuse planning can be understood through the use of patterns. Modeling the aspects of reuse at the highest level (e.g., enterprise) creates a template for reuse that can then introduce the concepts of reuse throughout the organization in a consistent manner.

Figure 7.2 is a top-level pattern that captures a best practice for model reuse. Four high-level subpatterns are modeled; pattern descriptions for each are provided. A high-level concept description for the metapattern is provided. The remainder of the chapters follows the format of the previous chapters.

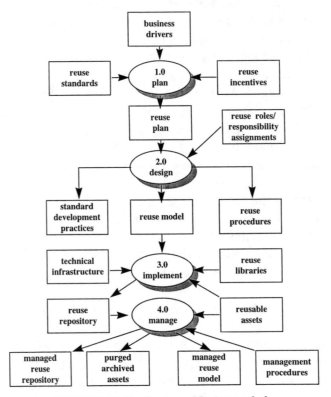

FIGURE 7.2. Reuse Metamodel

Reuse Metamodel: Pattern Description

1.0 *Plan* for reuse in the organization, using reuse incentives, standards and business drivers as components for inclusion in a reuse plan.

2.0 *Design* a reuse model, based on the reuse plan, incorporating standard development practices for technical architecture and application design, specific reuse procedures and reuse staff roles/responsibilities and assignments.

3.0 *Implement* reuse model, incorporating the technical infrastructure required to support reuse, and bringing the model and initial reuse libraries online. Populate repository with reusable assets.

4.0 *Manage* the repository and reuse model by maintaining management procedures (such as versioning control and security access and measuring and rewarding reuse), resulting in archived assets and a managed reuse model.

REUSE METAMODEL: CONCEPT DESCRIPTION (WITH EXAMPLES)

CONCEPT NAME	DEFINITION	POSSIBLE SOURCES AND FORMAT	EXAMPLE
Business Drivers	Business concepts/tools that would benefit from effective reuse.	Documented and non-documented (anecdotal) requirement.	"We seem to have a lot of redundancy in our business when it comes to writing proposals. We could benefit by enabling effective storage/retrieval and reuse of proposal templates...."
Reuse Standards	Organizationally mandated standards for reuse.	Standards, procedures, policies.	"All company press releases must contain the following language and format. . . ."
Reuse Incentives	Policies that encourage creative reuse, as opposed to "NIH syndrome."	Published company policy.	"For each modification/reuse of a preexisting C++ class from the corporate repository, effectively reused in a new and unique application, the programmer/analyst will receive 10 additional points toward the bonus plan . . ."

REUSE METAMODEL: CONCEPT DESCRIPTION (WITH EXAMPLES)

CONCEPT NAME	DEFINITION	POSSIBLE SOURCES AND FORMAT	EXAMPLE
Reuse Model (composed-of) — Reuse Plan — Technical Architecture Model — Reuse Role/ Responsibility Assignments — Reuse Procedures	A detailed action plan that addresses new roles, procedures and policies to support the goals and objectives outlined in the Reuse Plan.	Document.	"Our Reuse Model is comprehensive in addressing the tactical methods for achieving our reuse objectives over the next three years . . ."
Reuse Procedures	Procedures for reusing shared components, as well as making available newly developed or reconfigured components.	Document, part of Reuse Model.	"The DBA and object librarian shall coordinate check-in/check-out routines from the shared repository, as well as administer the security access authorization codes . . ."
Technical Infrastructure	Component of technical architecture pertaining to the physical underpinnings of the computing environment: networks, servers, databases, routers, mainframes, etc.	Physical environment.	"Our infrastructure will allow us to partition 5 GB on the development server for the new reuse libraries, and provide open access to the data warehouse via the network backbone for browsing . . ."

REUSE METAMODEL: CONCEPT DESCRIPTION (WITH EXAMPLES)

CONCEPT NAME	DEFINITION	POSSIBLE SOURCES AND FORMAT	EXAMPLE
Reuse Libraries	A subset (part-of) reusable assets.	Object code.	C++ class libraries
Reuse Repository (state-of) — Populated — Tested — Managed	A repository (database) that maintains storage of reusable concepts/tools, including design/analysis artifacts, code segments, documents, images, etc.	Database (object-oriented or capable of storing diverse data types).	"Our reuse repository is implemented with an object-oriented database, and is being populated with multiple data types—which will be important in realizing our reuse goals. Query and retrieval of data appears to be much faster traversing an object hierarchy . . ."
Reusable Assets	Any element that has the potential of ongoing value to an organization through reuse.	Patterns (KADS and design), documents, architectures, frameworks, code, intellectual property, designs.	"Any substantive deliverable to the business, be it a proposal, a design prototype, or a new estimating algorithm, has reuse potential and should treated as a reusable asset . . ."
Managed Reuse Repository	Reuse repository that is implemented, populated and maintained according to rules and criteria, including reuse tracking and archiving/purging of assets.	Database (object-oriented or capable of storing diverse data types).	"We are tracking an average of 27 instances of pattern reuse on a daily basis, and monitoring the controls for reuse incentive/ rewards . . ."

REUSE METAMODEL: CONCEPT DESCRIPTION (WITH EXAMPLES)

CONCEPT NAME	DEFINITION	POSSIBLE SOURCES AND FORMAT	EXAMPLE
Purged Archived Assets	Assets that have been purged from the active repository for reasons relating to obsolescence or replacement by new assets.	Patterns, documents, architectures, frameworks, code, intellectual property, designs.	"Our documents and designs relating to breadboard design have been purged from the active reuse repository, as we are no longer in that business line and have sold off all relevant assets pertaining to breadboard design to VChips, Inc., . . ."
Managed Reuse Model	The Reuse Model, in practice, as a living document.	Document.	"Several significant tactical adjustments have been necessitated in the Reuse Model over the past month, including . . ."
Management Procedures	Standard operating management procedures.	Management documents, meetings.	"Any expenditures over $5,000 must be pre-approved by the CFO, except under circumstances where . . ."

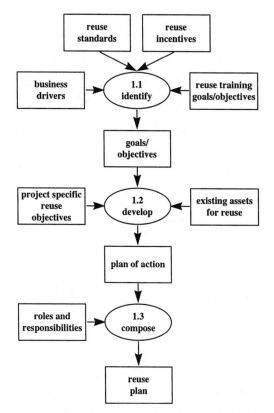

FIGURE 7.3. Subprocess 1.0: Plan for Reuse

Subpattern 1.0 (Plan for Reuse) Pattern Description

1.1 *Identify* goals and objectives for planning effort, based on the business drivers and previously agreed upon reuse standards, reuse incentives, and reuse training goals and objectives.

1.2 *Develop* plan of action based on goals and objectives, existing assets available for reuse, and project-specific reuse objectives.

1.3 *Compose* the reuse plan, incorporating the plan of action and roles and responsibilities.

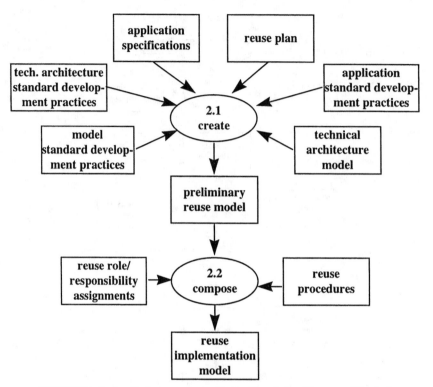

FIGURE 7.4. Subprocess 2.0: Design Reuse Model

Subpattern 2.0 (Design for Reuse) Pattern Description

2.1   Create the preliminary reuse model, based on reuse plan, the existing and planned technical-architecture design model, application specification(s), and the technical-architecture, model and application standard-development practices.

2.2   Compose the reuse implementation model, using the preliminary reuse model and incorporating reuse procedures and reuse role and responsibility assignments.

Subpattern 3.0 (Implement Reuse) Pattern Description

3.1   Implement reuse repository, based on the reuse implementation model and the technical infrastructure (e.g., software/hardware) required to support the reuse activities.

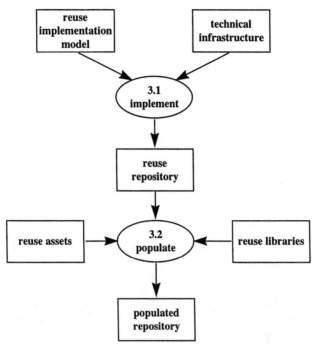

FIGURE 7.5. Subprocess 3.0: Implement Reuse Plan

3.2 *Populate* the reuse repository with reuse assets and applicable reuse libraries.

Subpattern 4.0 (Manage Reuse) Pattern Description

4.1 *Generalize/Test* the repository assets.

4.2 *Maintain* the tested assets using management procedures (e.g., QA and maintenance rules) as defined in the plan and procedures.

4.3 *Track* reuse of the repository assets, and maintain metrics for determining long-term business value of assets and reward incentives.

4.4 *Archive/Purge* the repository asset as necessary.

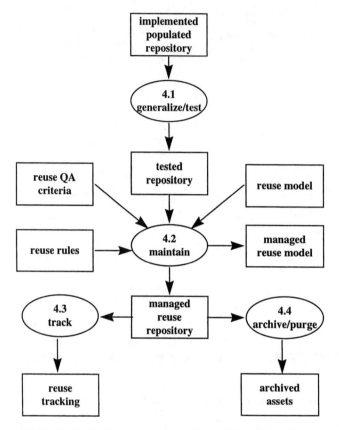

FIGURE 7.6. Subprocess 4.0: Manage Reuse

SUMMARY

The promise of object technology and patterns—component-based reassembling of reusable components—can only be achieved through reuse, and reuse can only be achieved through careful planning. The process of reusing patterns and objects is that of packaging knowledge as objects patterns, making them visible and accessible for reuse, and folding improved, used objects and patterns back into the whole process. The rewards of reuse can be phenomenal. However, these rewards build over time, following the volume of high-quality reusable objects/patterns available from a repository, library, or through a networked environment.

REFERENCES

Anderson, J. A. (Aug. 1990). *Technology Insertion: Establishing an Object-Oriented Life-Cycle Methodology.* Selected Papers on Object-Oriented Technology, CSC Technology Report 90-1.

Gamma, E., R. Helm, R. Johnson & J. Vlissides (1995). *Design Patterns: Elements of Reusable Object-Oriented Software.* Reading, MA: Addison-Wesley.

Griss, M. & W. Tracz, eds. (April 1993). *WISR92: 5th Annual Workshop on Software Reuse Working Group Reports,* Software Engineering Notes, 18 (2), ACM Sigsoft.

Hartman, M., F. W. Jewell, C. Scott & D. Thornton (1994). *Taking an Object-Oriented Methodology into the Real World. Papers.* AMA OOPSLA.

Margones, Yohan, et. al. (29 April 1994). *Volume 1: Guidebook for Building Cost-Effective Systems, Version 1.0.* CSC Consulting White Paper.

Martin, J. & J. Odell (1995). *Object-Oriented Methods: A Foundation.* Englewood Cliffs, NJ: Prentice-Hall.

McGregor, J. D. & D. A. Sykes (1992). *Object-Oriented Software Development: Engineering Software for Reuse.* New York: Van Nostrand Reinhold.

Objectory Corporation (Nov. 1994). *Reuse Strategies and Cross Project Team Development.* Objectory Corporation Brochure.

Rotella, P. (1994). *Managing an Object-Oriented Project Using an Interactive Approach.* AMA OOPSLA.

Tansley, D. & C. C. Hayball (1995). *Knowledge-Based Systems Analysis and Design: A KADS Developer's Handbook.* Englewood Cliffs, NJ: Prentice-Hall.

Vitalari, Nick (Chairman) & CSC Research and Advisory Services (Oct. 1994). *Object-Engineering Action Group Notes.* CSC Summit.

CHAPTER 8

Best Practice: Testing OO Systems

PURPOSE

The purpose of this chapter is to illustrate the use of KADS Patterns as a way to describe best-practice testing planning and procedures.

The development of moderate and large-scale distributed object-oriented (OO) systems involves the cooperative interaction of numerous individuals, including project managers, subject-matter experts, domain modelers, database designers, implementors and testers. Such systems are usually characterized by complex domains, changing sets of requirements, constrained dates for deliverables, hardware/software incompatibilities or other difficulties. Important to our understanding of building such systems is the role that testing plays.

It is surprising that the development of testing strategies and methods for OO systems is quite recent and somewhat untried, given that object technology itself is now twenty years old. Some organizations that have successfully used more traditional forms of testing may find these tried-and-true approaches inadequate for OO software-development efforts. The principle reason for this is that OO systems are inherently different and thus insert additional levels of complexity into the development process.

In part, the complexity is due to the nature of OO systems. The object modeling and programming paradigm is sometimes unfamiliar to both managers and their in-house development staff, requiring a shift in how systems are designed and constructed. Object-oriented programming concepts such as inheritance and polymorphism challenge testers to come up with more innovative methods for evaluating the functionality of these systems. Moreover, the creation of reusable software components, an advantage espoused by purveyors of the OO paradigm, is only achieved by validating and verifying the correctness of the design and testing the system's constituent parts. Complexity increases significantly in the testing of hybrid systems, which incorporate one or more legacy applications "wrapped" by objects.

There is no doubt that software testing is a valuable activity. In fact, untested or ill-tested software often leads to postponed release dates or that are errors unacceptable to the end-user. Even when testing occurs later in the life cycle it has been known to consume 40 percent or more of the initial software-development budget. Where budgets and time frames are constrained, testing activities are frequently reduced to such as extent that the reliability of the software is questionable. Poor or inadequate testing is one predictor of software failure.

Many organizations practice some kind of software testing. A few have instituted enterprise-wide testing strategies, while others have organized and carried out testing on a project-to-project basis. Without a doubt, some organizations would prefer not to do any testing at all and view it as a costly nuisance. Certainly, a good testing program is an investment in people, training and tools. It requires changes in the attitudes of management and staff toward software testing. It also requires commitment. The seemingly excessive costs that managers may first experience are more than negated by improved software quality and testing efficiency.

The motivation for developing a pattern-based approach for testing is threefold. First, we are interested in better understanding the testing process, as there are significant differences between OO and non-OO system testing. Second, we wish to identify a set of "best practices" for testing. Third, we want to map the testing process to the development life cycle. It is our contention that a continuous, iterative testing effort, started during the early stages of development, will help developers build reliable OO systems in a timely, cost-effective manner.

DEFINITION

Testing is the process by which software is formally and systematically probed for the presence of errors. This is a simple definition, yet much is implied. The term "process" means that there is an established set of procedures that are followed to achieve some end goal. The term "formally" connotes that the procedures have structure, either some aspects take place before others or they are performed in parallel. "Systematically" suggests that a strategy exists for "probing," or examining, the software. "Errors" are mistakes that result in coding faults, which in turn lead to software failures. Users of software notice failures. Testers attempt to identify the errors that lead to failures before the software is released.

Most errors found in software are introduced early in a project, particularly during the requirements phase. Some studies indicate that more than 50 percent of all errors are entered at this time. Since finding and correcting such errors are always more expensive during the latter portions of the development cycle, it behooves all project participants to identify and correct them at a much earlier stage. For these reasons, testing must be well managed and fully integrated into the entire development effort.

The approach toward testing is also affected by the development strategy. Several life-cycle approaches are currently used by developers. While some seem more in vogue than others, they include the sequential- and iterative-waterfall models, the spiral-development model, and the iterative/incremental model. Also included is RAD (rapid application development) and other variations, such as rapid evolutionary development and rapid prototyping. These latter methods, as their names imply, emphasize speedy software development.

Within the confines of these development structures are limitations on how a test team approaches the problem of testing software. For example, the sequential-waterfall model has testing taking place as the final activity. RAD, on the other hand, requires that most testing be conducted by the end-user, not by an independent test group. Spiral and iterative/incremental models revisit testing at iterative stages as more functionality is built into the system.

One last need is to clarify the concepts of testing software and debugging software. They are not at all the same. The discovery of errors is the principle purpose of testing. The root cause of the error is not the goal, only the fact that an error exists. Debugging is more concerned with finding and fixing the causes of the errors that testing uncovers.

THE BUSINESS CASE FOR A PATTERN APPROACH TO TESTING

A pattern approach has proven to be quite useful in developing testing strategies for OO systems. Developing OO software-testing frameworks based on patterns offers the following benefits:

- *A more complete understanding of the testing process:* A pattern approach provides a better understanding of the testing process as a whole by articulating in a more precise fashion what kinds of testing concepts and operations are relevant. One possible benefit is that the testing process may be streamlined by first examining and then modifying, if relevant, the relationships and interactions between the various testing activities.
- *A better match between the testing structure and business goals:* A pattern approach permits the development of a testing structure that more suitably matches the business. For example, an organization may contract out a portion of a software-development effort with the intention of expediting its completion and/or reducing costs. It is not uncommon in these instances for an existing testing structure to be out of sync with changing management objectives. A pattern approach can help to identify what aspects of testing are influenced by these changes and how the changes would affect overall software quality.
- *A more appropriate way of matching software design and functionality with specific OO test procedures:* Patterns delivers a more precise mapping of static and dynamic test procedures to those structural and behavioral characteristics of the software under test. The use of patterns leads to the development of test cases and tests scripts that exercise the targeted functionality and dependencies of classes and objects more rigorously. As a consequence, unnecessary or redundant tests may be omitted altogether.
- *A better approach for designing and selecting test cases for exercising systems:* A pattern approach allows testers to judiciously design and choose a set of test cases used to exercise various components of the system. For example, complex transactions that access several databases and/or spawn other subprocesses are both difficult to understand and test. Patterns permit a better comprehension of the transaction and thus lead to the construction and use of more suitable test cases.
- *An improved method for matching test tools and metrics with testing needs:* Finally, patterns help testers identify which test tools and metrics are most appropriate for their testing environment. There is a better understanding of why, for example, complexity metrics designed for non-OO code are inadequate for OO software. Such findings eliminate the need for certain types of testing tools.

SOFTWARE TESTING: TRADITIONAL VS. PATTERN APPROACH

Software testing, like software development in general, is a maturing discipline. Good testing procedures of a decade ago are now inadequate for the kinds of software systems constructed today. More traditional testing practices worked well when systems were rather simple and mainframes were the standard fare. Then, testing was generally carried out by developers, not specialists, who would compile, run and test individual software components or other software structures. The units, when completed, would be assembled or integrated together, usually one component at a time. More tests were carried out to insure that these assemblies worked properly. When all the components were compiled, the complete system would be tested in whole. For obvious reasons, the testing of these components and assemblies was commonly referred to as unit testing, integration testing, and system testing.

Software units are generally considered to be the smallest possible piece of software that can be tested in an independent manner. Some distinguishing characteristics of units are that they exist in separate files, they are compiled separately and in isolation, and they are typically small, consisting of less than a few hundred lines of code. In non-OO implementations, units are referred to as "modules" or "procedures." White-box, black-box and gray-box tests are suitable at this level. If interfaces exist, they are typically stubbed off.

Integration testing focuses on discovering errors and inconsistencies when units are brought together and recompiled. The point of doing this, of course, is to examine interfaces between other internal units or external components, such as other systems, databases, and input and output devices.

System testing examines the entire product for errors and deficiencies. Some test scripts can be exercised again to evaluate the total functioning of the system. New test scripts are designed and executed as well to evaluate the behavior of other system characteristics. System testing is mostly black-box.

The pattern approach differs from more traditional approaches for testing software because, in part, it is model based. Models are structures that aid human understanding. There are many kinds of models, ranging from simple drawings and graphs to explicit mathematical constructs. Common to each is the attempt by modelers to simplify seemingly complex representations. KADS Object, when viewed from this perspective, is a modeling technique that renders a cognitive representation of the patterns found in testing processes.

The pattern approach is also distinguished from more traditional testing approaches by exploring the "what," not the "how," of testing. How software is tested is important, but it is an implementation issue and varies from organization to organization, or even from project to project. The "what" allows testers to focus on elements or concepts that comprise good testing practices.

Thus a pattern approach leads to a tighter mapping of testing to the software-development life cycle. It also permits individuals who are designing or redesigning testing procedures to more readily identify and include business objectives into the process. Furthermore, a pattern perspective is a more natural fit for object-oriented software designs and is a better mechanism for constructing static and dynamic tests of distributed OO systems.

The differences between traditional testing approaches and the KADS approach are shown in table 8.1.

BEST-PRACTICE PATTERN: SOFTWARE TESTING

Testing consists of several related processes, which are listed below. At first glance, the listing may imply that the processes are carried out in order. This is not the case. While it is true that having a test team in place must occur before any other activity, in practice, many of the processes are conducted in parallel:

- organizing the high-level strategy;
- selecting appropriate test tools;
- developing iterative tests;
- developing test plans;
- constructing test cases and scripts;
- exercising the tests;

TABLE 8.1. Traditional Testing Approaches Vs. KADS Approaches

Traditional Approach	KADS Approach
Non-model based	Model based
Focus on the "how" of testing	Focus on the "what" of testing
Mapping of testing to software development life cycle <u>not</u> clearly articulated	Mapping of testing to software development life cycle clearly articulated
Business objectives which influence testing <u>not</u> apparent	Business objectives which influence testing identified
Emphasis of testing software modules or procedures	Emphasis on testing software objects that participate in specific patterns

• collecting and analyzing test results;
• reporting the results.

SOFTWARE TESTING METAMODEL

The software testing metapattern is presented figure 8.1, followed by its pattern description and concept description. Two subpatterns (6.0 and 7.0) are then further detailed.

Software Testing Metamodel: Pattern Description

1.0 *Organize* the high-level strategy.
In an iterative, incremental development environment, organizing a high-level strategy is critical for the successful implementation of any testing program. The enterprise testing policy provides general guidelines and defines expectations for software testing within the organization. Management objectives influence the

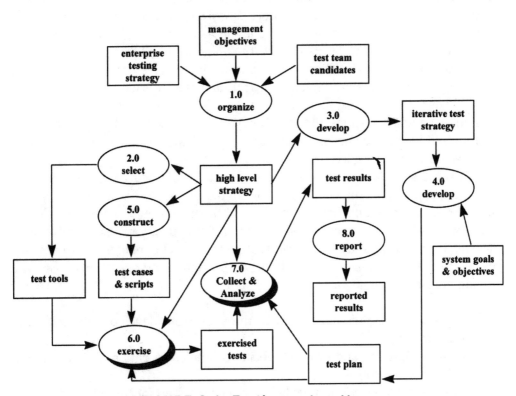

FIGURE 8.1. Testing metapattern

manner and degree to which testing activities are undertaken. Test-team members are also identified at this time. The result is the development of a high-level strategy that describes aspects of testing such as staffing and schedules.

Among the different organizational activities described in a high-level strategy, forming a test team is extremely important. Organizing a test team means that the required expertise for a given project fits the skill set of selected test-team members. The test team is thus composed of individuals who are categorized into four roles: team lead, subject-matter experts (SMEs), testers, and, on occasion, test advocates. The size of the test team is dependent upon the size of the project and the collective skill set of individual test-team members.

The basic role of the test-team lead is to guide the overall testing effort. This individual has previous experience in software testing. The test leader's responsibility includes delegating work to other team members, developing and updating test plans, and participating in project meetings. The team leader should provide information to project management.

An equally important role is that of the SME who has intimate knowledge about the business domain. SMEs typically are the source of information for designers and modelers. Large OO projects work with several SMEs, so it is not unexpected that more than one SME may be required to assist on a test team. The primary function of SMEs on a test team is to help design and create test scenarios and test cases. They ensure that business rules are correctly implemented, correct events are fired and proper data are returned.

In sheer numbers, testers comprise the largest segment of the testing staff. Testers have many responsibilities and have been trained in the use of specific test tools. If specialized test programs are required, the testers are the ones most likely to develop the code.

In some situations, testing advocates, because of their specialized knowledge and experience, may be helpful for limited periods of time. Depending on how development teams are structured and before testing begins, it would be valuable to identify personnel who can act in the capacity of testing advocate. The testing advocate is a member of a subsystem development team who works closely with the test team to evaluate the performance and operation of the system in question. The advocate can:

- act as a point-of-contact between the subsystem development team and the test team;
- identify, describe and provide specific examples of data required as input values for the subsystem;
- provide a full description of the interfaces required for the subsystem;

- review unit and integration test plans for the subsystem;
- build, where necessary, custom code to capture and store the origin and destination of messages passed between objects in order to more quickly identify the source of a particular fault or error;
- act as a resource for the test team when determining the boundary conditions of the test cases at the system test level.

2.0 *Select* test tools to automate the testing process.

This operation is guided by the high-level testing strategy and is critical for successful software testing. Choices for testing tools depend upon the availability of the tool for a particular software-development environment, its cost, and any previous experience testers might have had with it.

Many automated tools are now available that support software testing. The fact that these tools are automated does not imply their ease of use. Nevertheless, a commitment by management to properly train users is required as the tools can provide significant gains in the time needed to adequately test software. Testing tools are available for most of the common operating systems and platforms.

Tools for object-oriented system development can be divided into several categories. They include stand-alone testing tools like the **McCabe Object-Oriented Tool** or **OOMetric**, which provides measurements for the structural attributes of object-oriented code; **Purify**, which is used to detect memory leaks; and **X-Simultest**, a GUI test tool. Some products, such as **OMT**, provide built-in testing features (automated script generation for code coverage; OO metrics) into their environments. Others, like Centerline's **TestCenter,** incorporate several tools under a single license for measuring compile and run-time performances and providing debugging capabilities. A few tools directly support programmers while others are intended for use by members of a test team. Although not strictly limited to OO development, **PureDTTs** or **Defect Control System** are important tools for reporting and tracking software defects.

3.0 *Develop* iterative tests for the testing activity.

Iterative testing refers to tests carried out at different stages of the software-development life cycle. For example, in an iterative test environment, testing takes place during phases of requirement gathering, design and modeling, and coding. Further tests are conducted when the components of the software are integrated into larger assemblages or into the final system. In iterative/incremental development, some of these stages are revisited, necessitating strategies for conducting regression testing. Iterative testing is influenced by the goals and objectives of the high-level strategy.

Iterative testing begins with the pattern models of KADS Object. These patterns consist of concepts, concept hierarchies, problem-solving templates and pattern descriptions. Concepts in isolation are not testable in the usual sense. They are either deemed important, as in core business concepts, or unimportant, where they may be discarded in subsequent analyses.

Concepts are testable only from the perspective of their relationship with each other. Concept hierarchies, for example, represent this relationship. Like code walk-throughs, a designer may chose to participate in concept walk-throughs where relationships like "is-a," "attribute" and "composed-of" are checked. In addition, the concepts in the hierarchies can be shown to be necessary (or not) by their participation in a specific "operation."

KADS Object templates are testable in two ways. First, the diagrams are testable in the sense that one needs to show that only necessary and sufficient conditions hold for the diagram to be accurate. Necessity implies that a condition must be met. Sufficiency means that only certain conditions are required, not any more. For example, it can be demonstrated that for a given output from a particular operation, only specific inputs are necessary. Second, KADS patterns are also tested by requiring SMEs to examine each in detail. This makes sense as the SMEs are the primary source from which the patterns were derived. Patterns should be checked for correctness, completeness and consistency. Logical walk-throughs of the patterns using test data (concept examples or instances) with the SMEs is a simple yet highly effective means of testing the model.

As been shown in previous chapters, the mapping of KADS models to OO models is tightly bound (e.g., concept hierarchies to objects, relationships between objects, and object attributes). Scenarios can be developed and then run to validate the object representation for SMEs and other domain experts. Case tools like **LiveModel** from IntelliCorp automate this kind of effort. Once the models are validated at this level, implementation can be initiated. As code is created, more formalized testing procedures are followed.

Concepts, hierarchies and KADS diagrams, if constructed properly, represent user requirements and specifications. Since many errors are introduced during requirements gathering, it behooves testers and users alike to closely examine the KADS patterns and subsequent use cases and OQ representations before coding activities take place.

Many modeling tools generate code, primarily C++. Testing at this level becomes more specific. It includes static and dynamic tests performed at the time of unit, integration and system-testing phases. Static tests are usually undertaken with the help of testing tools. Dynamic tests sometimes require the development of specialized objects called monitors, which capture run-time behavioral aspects of the system. Static and dynamic tests are discussed later in this chapter.

4.0 *Develop* the test plan.

The test plan is a formal statement about the goals and procedures for conducting software tests. The plan is influenced by the goals and objectives of the system under development and the iterative test strategy. In some organizations, the test plan is limited in design and scope. For others, the plan is quite elaborate. The test plan may vary in focus as well, with a single general plan outlining the major testing objectives of the project and more specific plans for other testing activities, such as integration testing. General test plans should address the project's software development environment, hardware requirements and testing standards. Personnel, schedules and tools are usually described at this level.

It is sometimes advantageous to develop more specific test plans for each development iteration. The objectives of these plans should be clearly defined and should include a list of the test cases that will exercise the desired behavior of the system. They should also identify and describe the sets of process and product metrics applicable for the system under test.

Process metrics are those that relate to the way in which an organization develops software. Process metrics might track the kinds and frequency of software errors or the severity level of the error. Process metrics are beyond the scope of this discussion (although they appear in figure 8.3 as QA Metrics). Nevertheless, several references are cited in the bibliography, should the reader have interest in this area (Beizer, 1994; Hetzel, 1993; Shepperd, 1993). It is sufficient to state that measuring process will lead to improvements in the quality of the product and the development environment.

Product metrics help to measure the static (design) and dynamic (behavioral) characteristics of the system. The focus here, however, is on metrics related to software and more specifically, to OO software. Such software is described in terms of classes, objects and methods, not procedures, subprograms or functions that have dominated legacy system development. The difference in nomenclature is significant. One can have several objects operating in concert that perform a single function or one object that carries out multiple functions. This mind-set is not altogether difficult to understand, but for some organizations the transitioning to an object-oriented way of thinking is not without its own set of problems.

Static metrics are those that describe design characteristics of the code. Six specific metrics for which sound mathematical foundations have been established have been identified (Chidamber, 1994), and are recommended for use by test teams. Note that the categories of metrics differ significantly from that of procedurally-coded software.

- Weighted Methods per Class: the sum of the number of methods and complexity of methods for a class; used as a predictor of the time and effort needed to develop and maintain the class.
- Depth of Inheritance: a measure of the number of ancestor classes that can affect a class; deeper trees indicate greater design complexity.
- Number of Children: a measure of the number of subclasses that inherit the methods of the parent; large numbers of children are indicators of the potential for reuse or suggest the need for greater testing.
- Coupling between Object Classes: a count of the number of couplings of one class with others; excessive coupling prevents reuse, increases maintenance efforts and requires more rigorous testing.
- Response for a Class: a count of the set of methods that can be invoked in response to the arrival of a message to an object of this class; larger counts are indicative of the need for greater testing and debugging.
- Lack of Cohesion of Methods: the count of the number of disjoint method pairs minus similar method pairs in a class; indicates that a class should be split up into two or more subclasses; cohesiveness promotes encapsulation.

Other metrics have been suggested as well, but these lack the mathematical rigor of those identified above. Some of these metrics are listed below. Descriptions are found elsewhere (Lorenz & Kidd, 1994).

- Number of message sends;
- Number of public instance methods;
- Method complexity;
- Number of instance variables;
- Number of class methods;
- Number of class variables;
- Multiple inheritance;
- Number of methods overridden;
- Number of methods inherited;
- Class cohesion;

• Number of system or class globals;
• Class reuse.

"Dynamic metrics" refer to measurements taken at run-time. These metrics are more difficult to capture, often requiring specialized code that monitors the interaction of objects. Possible run-time measurements might evaluate the kinds and frequency of messages being sent to and from an object, determine the frequency that certain operations invoked or examine the changes taking place in the state of a particular object. Most dynamic metrics collected today are related to system performance.

A class of metrics that would be of immense value are complexity metrics. The concept of complexity metrics is not new—the Halsted and McCabe complexity metrics are well known. However, they were developed for non-OO systems and are not sufficient for object-oriented development efforts. The new class of complexity metrics needs to address the interoperability of objects that function in a distributed environment. Complexity metrics might address computational or cognitive aspects of the system.

5.0 *Construct* test cases and scripts.

The construction of test cases and scripts is affected by the high-level strategy. Proper testing requires the construction of test cases that, when executed, exercise the system in specific ways. Test cases are constructed with requirements in mind and explicitly describe the expected results. Test cases document the execution conditions for the item under test. They are influenced by the high-level strategy.

Test cases are usually represented in tabular form. As in the more traditional testing approaches, each test case requires a unique identification. In OO implementations, however, it is necessary to identity the class that is executed (or if testing interdependencies, the set of classes), its state, and any methods that may be invoked. This becomes particularly important for core classes such as "Customer" or "Account," which form the foundation for many business operations. Expected results for the test should be presented.

If applicable, exceptions, interrupts and external conditions should be exercised as well. Comments should be recorded if necessary.

6.0 *Exercise* the tests.

In a broad sense, OO systems are tested in similar fashion to non-OO systems. That is, test plans are created, appropriate tools are selected to support the automation of testing activities, test scripts are built, selected tests are performed and results are summarized and disseminated to the developers who then debug the errors and make changes to the code. If necessary, specialized test drivers can be built by testers to exercise files of input values and capture resulting discrepancies. The high-level strategy guides the overall testing effort.

The specifics of testing OO systems, however, differ significantly from traditional approaches. For one, the object state will affect the manner in which test cases are designed and executed. Secondly, encapsulation shifts the focus of testing from the module or subprogram to the object, which, in turn, directly impacts how much integration testing is necessary if coding changes are made. Thirdly, inheritance greatly influences the development of test cases and test scripts.

For example, consider an object called "Customer," which may have the states "New," "Existing," or "Former." A method, such as "Check-Customer-Credit-Limit" may apply to each of these states. Different test cases may be required for the method given the state of "Customer." Since "Customer" is encapsulated, it can be tested in isolation. Nevertheless, several new test cases may be required to fully exercise the interaction between "Customer" and other objects, such as "Account." If "Customer" inherits a method from its parent, other test cases may be needed to determine if that inherited method functions as planned.

7.0 *Collect and Analyze* the test results.

This operation is affected by the high-level strategy, the test plan, and the exercised tests. The most obvious reason is that errors discovered during testing must be traceable to particular test cases and scripts and then analyzed to determine the cause of the error.

Collecting measurements that help guide the design and implementation of the system also are of immense value. These measurements are numeric representations of the overall software-development process and the software products that are created by it. Collection of various measurements for collection sake is not the objective; rather, the measurements are indicators of the development process and provide guidance to developers and modelers who are concerned about design and behavioral attributes of individual software components. The types of process metrics collected by the organization are identified by the high-level strategy.

8.0 *Report* the results.

This operation requires that a reporting strategy be in place when testing reveals errors. Reports should be prepared at the end of each testing phase and disseminated to project managers and developers as appropriate.

SOFTWARE TESTING METAMODEL: CONCEPT DESCRIPTION (WITH EXAMPLES)

CONCEPT NAME	DEFINITION	POSSIBLE SOURCES AND FORMAT	EXAMPLE
Management Objectives	Management objectives specific to a project, and testing associated with that project. Management may express some variance on the criticality of testing from case to case.	Documents; written and verbal expressions.	"This project is viewed as mission-critical, and must undergo rigorous testing throughout development. Senior management therefore supports any additional staff or schedule adjustments on this initiative to ensure thorough testing . . ."
Enterprise Testing Policy	Organizational policies, procedures, or documented objectives pertaining to testing.	Policy documents.	"All software deployed in our production environment must undergo, at a minimum, unit, integration and system testing and be certified by the QA department . . ."
Test Team Candidates	Candidate staff to fill roles designated for testing. Role categories include team lead, subject-matter expert, testers and test advocates.	Part of test plan.	"Test-team candidates have been identified in the attached list. Role assignments will be designated based on availability and supervisors' approval . . ."

SOFTWARE TESTING METAMODEL: CONCEPT DESCRIPTION (WITH EXAMPLES)

CONCEPT NAME	DEFINITION	POSSIBLE SOURCES AND FORMAT	EXAMPLE
Iterative Test Strategy	Schedule for ongoing testing, which is carried out throughout the development life cycle.	Part of test plan.	"Builds and unit testing for components A–E will occur twice weekly, according to the following schedule . . ."
High-Level Strategy	High-level view of the testing process for a project, based on available resources, etc. Strategy may be adjusted iteratively based on test results. The high-level strategy guides the overall testing effort.	Documents, status reports.	"Unit testing has proceeded ahead of schedule for components B and C. Recommend we move ahead on integration testing for those component . . ."
Test Tools	Commercial testing tools.	Software.	"We are using a set of commercial tools for testing various aspects of the system, including LoadRunner, Purify and X-Simultest . . ."

SOFTWARE TESTING METAMODEL: CONCEPT DESCRIPTION (WITH EXAMPLES)

CONCEPT NAME	DEFINITION	POSSIBLE SOURCES AND FORMAT	EXAMPLE
Test Cases & Scripts	Testing scenarios recorded as Cases (large-grained functions) and Scripts (fine-grained scenarios that exercise specific instances and rules).	Documentation, code, test data.	"Test script #12 will test the online balance inquiry function, for a retail customer who's credit card balance has less than $50 available credit . . ."
Test Results (composed-of) — Actual test results — differences (from expected results)	Test results are recorded after collection and analysis, comparing actual results with expected results.	Documentation, reports.	Expected result of script #12 was a warning pop-up dialog, indicating that available credit was low. Test did not fire the low credit rule, which in turn invokes the pop-up warning. Instead, credit balances (correct amounts) were displayed . . ."
System Goals & Objectives	System goals and objectives incorporated into the development of the test plan, to ensure everything works and performs according to specification, and meets the original intent.	Documentation.	"The system should allow 7X24 access, and should be able to process up to 300 simultaneous inquiries with under 7 seconds of response time . . ."

SOFTWARE TESTING METAMODEL: CONCEPT DESCRIPTION (WITH EXAMPLES)

CONCEPT NAME	DEFINITION	POSSIBLE SOURCES AND FORMAT	EXAMPLE
Exercised Tests (invoked-by) - test script - test tool - test driver	Test cases and scripts that have been run, and whose results are being analyzed.	Documentation, code, test data.	"All test scripts within test case #6 have been run in the a.m. batch cycles, and are available for analysis . . ."
Reported Results	Test results that have been analyzed and distilled into meaningful reports.	Reports.	"Testing of online functions currently does not meet performance goals. Although the system functionality and business logic is testing through cleanly, simulated transactions that exceed 240 simultaneous have response times in the 10–12 second range . . ."
Test Plan	The document which identifies and guides all testing activities for a project, including schedules, tests, tools, personnel, etc.	Document.	"Our test plan document includes the following major sections in Table of Contents: General Testing Guidelines Specific Testing Guidelines Testing Metrics Testing Tools Certification Recommendations

The testing metamodel indicates two operations that are drilled down in greater detail: ***Exercise*** and ***Collect and Analyze***. The first operation, ***Exercise*** *the test,* is shown as a KADS subpattern in figure 8.2. The second operation, ***Collect and Analyze*** *the test results,* is depicted in figure 8.3 as a subpattern.

Subpattern 6.0 (Exercise the Test) Pattern Description

6.1. ***Select*** tests that are appropriate given the test plan and available test cases and test scripts.

6.2. ***Select*** from the set of available test tools those that will meet the objectives of the tests as described in the test plan.

6.3. ***Match*** the selected tests to the appropriate test tool.

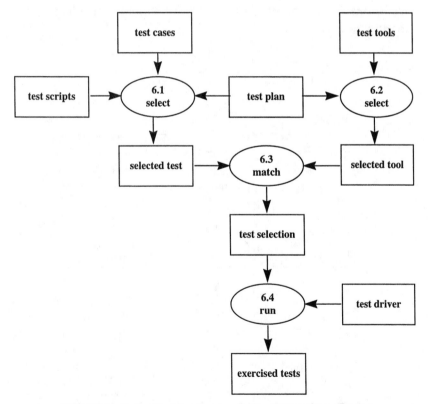

FIGURE 8.2. Subpattern 6.0: Exercise Tests

6.4.   **Run** the tests, using any necessary test drivers (programs or scripts developed to automatically supply input values to the class or classes under test).

Subpattern 7.0 (Collect and Analyze Test Results)
Pattern Description
The pattern description is as follows:

7.1.   **Collect** test results and quality-assurance metrics from the set of exercised tests described in the test plan. The test results and QA metrics should be stored in a repository for later retrieval and analysis.

7.2.   **Analyze** the QA metrics using standard analytical techniques, such as summary statistics, graphs, and charts.

7.3.   **Compare** the actual test results with the expected results in order to identify any differences.

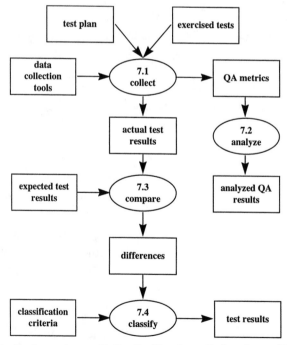

FIGURE 8.3. Subprocess 7.0: Collect and Analyze Test Results

7.4. *Classify* the difference of the test results based on classification criteria, such as error type or error severity.

SUMMARY

Before any testing of implemented code is undertaken, the test team should have in place entrance and exit criteria by which they are willing to accept models and code for test or release it for the next development iteration. For example, testers should have assurances from developers that the units (objects) are free of memory leaks and that boundary conditions have been thoroughly exercised before integration testing begins. Exit criteria for integration testing might include external interface functionality tests, for example.

The establishment of a metrics database would also help the test team. A metrics database would allow test-team members quick access to measurements collected during various phases of testing. Some automated test tools support this functionality, but full analytical capability is not always available.

Testing is also related to other kinds of activities that fall under the rubric of performance engineering. These types of tests are undertaken whether or not the desired system is an object-oriented system or a more traditional variant. They include:

- Performance tests: designed to show how well performance requirements are met.
- Timing tests: result in a collection of measurements that evaluate the flow of transactions across the required system components in an effort to identify bottlenecks.
- Stress tests: generally designed to place high transaction loads on a system in order to saturate system resources to a point where they fail.
- Platform tests: conducted to evaluate required system administrative functions such as equipment setup, kernel configuration, hardware and software upgrading, logging, and report generation.

Each of these kinds of tests are usually undertaken by a group outside the development environment and will not be described here.

The patterns presented here are a reflection of our view of testing as it applies to object-oriented system development. Ideally, testing is a continuous activity conducted to provide an organization with methods for developing working, user-accepted systems, and providing a means for generating classes of reusable software components. The models were developed with this in mind.

The following are general steps recommended to establish an adequate testing protocol.

1. At project initiation, designate a test lead. This individual can be selected from the client organization or may be brought in as a consultant. The test lead should have practical experience in organizing and conducting a testing program for large-scale systems.
2. Staff the test team with individuals who have practical knowledge of OO system development, not simply coders who have programmed in C++.
3. Establish roles and responsibilities for developers and testing team. For example, as developers have intimate knowledge of their own code, on some projects it would be appropriate that they be responsible for all unit testing. The test team should provide guidelines in these cases for designing test scripts, suggesting coverage and path test options, developing exit criteria for the unit tested code and the like. Depending on the extent to which design patterns are used, someone should have the responsibility for "certifying" design patterns.
4. Designate points of contact, if necessary, between the development teams and the test teams. As testing continues, testing advocates may be identified from within the ranks of the development team in order to assist testers during key stages of the testing effort.
5. Determine tool requirements based on project objectives (e.g., if no GUI is required, a GUI testing tool will not be needed). Ensure the availability of the tools to the test team and provide training if needed.
6. Provide input to the requirement definition team. Most errors are introduced at this time. Early detection of requirement errors will prevent problems later.
7. Develop the overall system test plan as early as possible. The system test plan is the detailed outline for all testing activities. At appropriate stages, enhance or modify the system test plan and develop additional plans for other general tests such as those related to integration or performance.
8. Build test cases and test scripts based on specific project objectives. Reference these test cases to system requirements, specifications, use-case descriptions, KADS hierarchies and the like.
9. Exercise the test scripts as needed. Develop test drivers where appropriate to expedite the testing effort and employ automated testing tools. Provide a mechanism or have in hand a tool for reporting the types and severity of errors encountered.

10. Conduct regression tests on code units that are reintroduced by the development team after changes have been made. Reuse existing scripts as appropriate.

Following these recommendation does not necessarily guarantee a successful project. The primary predictor of a successful testing effort is buy-in by project management on the value and importance of testing activities. This is achieved through the collection and analysis of metrics related to both the software and the process by which the software is generated. KADS patterns aid this process by providing a more thoroughly understood framework for testing software.

REFERENCES

Arthur, L. (1993). *Rapid Evolutionary Development*. NY: Wiley.

Beizer, B. (1994). *Software System Testing and Quality Assurance*. NY: Van Nostrand Reinhold.

Berard, E. (1993). *Essays on Object-Oriented Software Engineering*, Vol. 1. Englewood Cliffs, NJ: Prentice-Hall.

Chidamber, S. (1994). *Metrics for Object Oriented Software Design*. Ph.D. Diss. Alfred P. Sloan School of Management, Massachusetts Institute of Technology.

Hetzel, B. (1993). *Making Software Measurement Work*. Boston: QED Publishing Group.

Kit, E. (1995). *Software Testing in the Real World*. NY: Addison-Wesley.

Lorenz, M. & J. Kidd (1994). *Object-Oriented Software Metrics*. Englewood Cliffs, NJ: Prentice-Hall..

Martin, J. (1991). *Rapid Application Development*. NY: Macmillan.

Musa, J., A. Iannino & K. Okumoto (1987). *Software Reliability: Measurement, Prediction, Application*. NY: McGraw-Hill.

Shepperd, M. (1993). *Software Engineering Metrics Volume I: Measures and Validations*. London: McGraw-Hill.

Tansley, D. & C. Hayball (1993). *Knowledge-Based Systems Analysis and Design, A KADS Developer's Handbook*. Englewood Cliffs, NJ: Prentice-Hall.

CHAPTER 9

Case Study: A Retail Banking Example

INTRODUCTION

This chapter presents an end-to-end case study, which ties together the KADS pattern framework and techniques covered in the preceding chapters: defining cognitive approaches and understanding the business case, as well as specific applications of pattern modeling relating to object-oriented design, technical architecture and application development. This chapter will describe the pattern framework that binds the various aspects of an OO project together, in the context of a case study for a large retail bank. The case study is based on an actual engagement with a banking client that will be referred to as First Western Bank.

BACKGROUND

The Quality Assurance (QA) Division of First Western Bank initiated a project with the goal of improving their software-testing processes in terms of both quality and testing turnaround time. Specifically, the approach focused on current practices pertaining to the creation and setup of test data, and the desire to streamline those tasks by leveraging the use of data from the production environment for testing.

The *test data sampling* (*TDS*) application was proposed to assist First Western testing staff in selecting and assembling sets of production data from various First Western production databases. With 300–400 changes to production systems occurring weekly, the business case for streamlining the testing process was great. Also, given the limited window of opportunity for time-to-market of new banking services, testing was often not given adequate attention. The proposed application would reduce the amount of time needed to test (or increase the amount of available testing time) by quickly identifying test data based on criteria selected by testers.

First Western also recognized the value in approaching the modeling and development aspects of the TDS application from a cognitive perspective. The reasons for this were twofold:

1. *The selection of test data and development of test conditions and scripts was largely a cognitive process*, and one that was performed within the bank by only a small cadre of experts. Cognitive pattern modeling was identified as an approach that would enable knowledge capture and modeling of the deeply embedded expertise associated with the development of test sets for retail banking operations.

2. *Knowledge relating to the interdependencies of First Western's production environment was also limited to a small group of experts*. The mainframe environment had expanded over more than twenty years to accommodate ever increasing volumes. The legacy environment maintained many data and application couplings that were not well documented or understood. These interdependent couplings were viewed as very complex, and would require a modeling approach to manage that complexity in order to perform the production data extracts for the TDS application. Once again, the use of patterns was offered as an approach that would help mitigate the risk associated with modeling this highly complex environment.

PROJECT STRUCTURE

The TDS application was structured in two initial phases, with each phase timeboxed and unique in scope and deliverables. The project structure was intended to provide First Western Bank with tangible business value throughout the development life cycle, culminating in a deployed scalable prototype, with complete detailed KADS Object models supporting application and technical architecture. The first two time-boxed phases were intended to provide First Western with a rapid implementation, built upon an open, extensible architectural framework based on the use of patterns.

Each phase was timeboxed at three months, and defined as follows:

- **Phase I:** Phase one covered initial KADS Object modeling of the problem space, including a breakdown of the major patterns in the Quality Assurance Division. Major patterns were further refined to a second tier, and for those subpatterns presumed to fall within initial scope of the TDS application, a third tier was modeled. In addition, initial object modeling was performed using the Unified Modeling Language (UML) and Use Case notation, and conceptual architecture for TDS was developed in parallel to these activities.
- **Phase II:** Phase two included detailed design and implementation of a scalable prototype of TDS. The initial prototype deliverable was limited in scope to a few specific functional requirements. Major work activities included modeling (KADS, Use Case and Sequence Diagram) of a specific set of patterns and subpatterns for the prototype, and development of the logical/physical constrained architecture.

In addition to phases one and two, a third time-boxed development phase was planned and budgeted for, with the expectation that success within the first two phases would warrant scaling up TDS to include full functionality. Details of the phase three work plan were deferred until completion of phases one and two. Figure 9.1 shows an outline of the three phases of the TDS project.

KADS Model Development

In order to put the TDS application into a framework consistent with the objectives of the QA Division at First Western Bank, a top-level KADS diagram was constructed (figure 9.2) with the collaboration of several First Western testing analyst *domain experts*. The KADS diagram below in figure 9.2 indicates the metapattern

TDS Project Plan

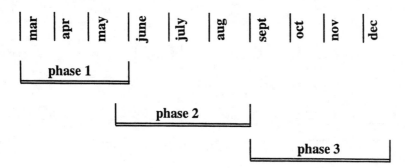

FIGURE 9.1. TDS Project Plan

(eight operations), and was the result of several iterations and consensus-building work sessions over a ten-day period. The definition of eight top-level operations/subpatterns is consistent with our experience that human cognition (and a guideline rule of KADS modeling) tends to abstract concepts into groups of six to ten. Examples of library templates that played a role in this system include: configuration, planning, modification, and classification.

Metapattern Description

1.0 *Review* and input business requirements into preliminary specifications (user and system), from the impact statement, business requirements and business work order.

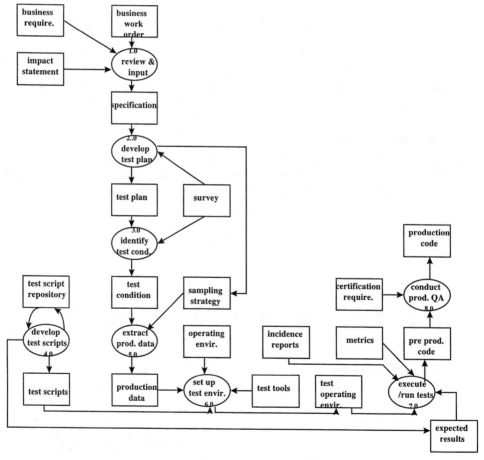

FIGURE 9.2. TDS Metapattern

2.0 *Develop* integration test plan from the specifications.

3.0 *Identify* the test conditions from the integration test plan, surveys and impact statements, in order to provide the test data selection criteria.

4.0 *Develop* test scripts from the test conditions, leveraging reuse through a (future state) shared test-script repository.

5.0 *Extract* production test data based on test-data selection criteria as well as the (future state) sampling strategy in the integration test plan.

6.0 *Setup* the test environment incorporating the pretested application code, test scripts and data, and necessary testing tools. This task includes all the necessary operational setup for test bank, as well as any nontest bank environment preparation (e.g., credit card testing).

7.0 *Execute/run* tests in the test-ready environment, according to the schedule in the integration test plan.

8.0 *Implement* tested code into production environment, and complete all post-installation QA as necessary (i.e., regression testing).

For the scalable TDS application, it was determined that detailed modeling of subpatterns would be required in parts of operations 3, 4 and 5. Those operations were defined by the QA Division testing analysts as areas containing the core functionality for the TDS application. Additional specialized domain expertise was identified for development of the KADS models for operations 3, 4 and 5.

Figure 9.3 shows the major second tier subpatterns that were modeled for all major operations 1 through 8 in the QA Division. Additional modeling detail to the third and fourth tier was undertaken for operations 3, 4 and 5 in order to deliver granularity necessary for detailed design and prototyping in phase two.

This diagram illustrates the subpatterns in 3, 4 and 5 that were modeled in finer detail for phase one of TDS. Specifically, subpattern 3.6 will be the subject of further examples in this case study. These models were developed over a two-week period, with frequent iterations and revisions, and consensus building on the concept definitions.

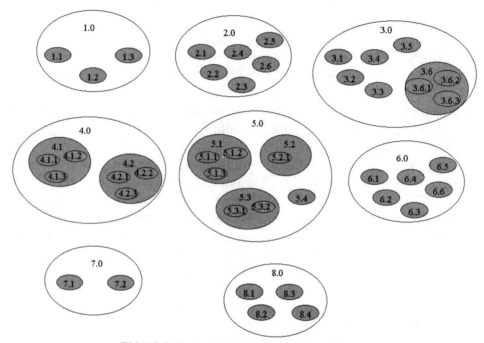

FIGURE 9.3. TDS Major Subpatterns

Requirements Definition

The requirements definition for the TDS application is based upon requirements driven from operations within the patterns defined in the KADS Object cognitive models. Use-case analysis based upon the KADS Object models were developed to support detailed design of the requirements in phase two.

Figure 9.4 shows a drilled-down detail model of process 3.6, along with corresponding system requirements.

3.6 Pattern Description

3.6.1 *Open* a new or existing test suite from the TDS repository.

3.6.2 *Create* a new test suite by inputting a new test suite i.d. and description to the TDS .

3.6.3 *Select* an existing test suite from the TDS repository by selecting from a list of test-suite ids.

3.6.4 *Browse/modify/delete* a test suite from the repository.

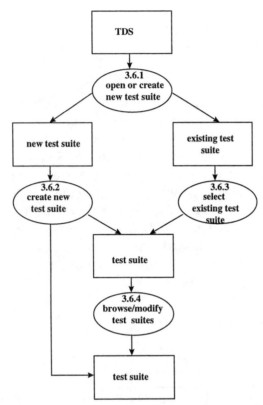

FIGURE 9.4. Process 3.6: Enter Suites, Scripts and Conditions

Object Model

Initial Object models (static object diagrams and sequence diagram) were created from mapping the concept hierarchies in the KADS models to the appropriate class definition in the object model. Class/concept abstractions in the KADS model should map to roughly the same level of detail in the object model. For example, the metaconcept "Production Data" in the top-level diagram is defined in a domain hierarchy as having an "is-a" relationship with the concepts "Customer," "Account" and "Service," as in the following example:

```
Production Data (is-a)
      Customer
      Account
          RTS
          Brokerage
          Credit Card
```

```
Service
     Safe Deposit
     Express Card
     Channel
```

These concepts are then incorporated in a meaningful way in second tier sub-diagrams, and are further refined into a number of distinct subtypes in sub-sub diagrams. Figure 9.5 illustrates the levels of abstraction of the concepts in the example above in their corresponding KADS diagrams. The top-level concept, "Production Data," logically appears in the top level diagram. The second tier concepts, "Account," "Service" and "Customer," logically appear in the second-tier diagram, and so on. The following three figures illustrate the concept abstractions represented in the KADS and object diagrams.

Figures 9.6 and 9.7 show the major class types and associations mapped from detailed modeling of patterns 3.0, 4.0 and 5.0. These classes are represented in UML.

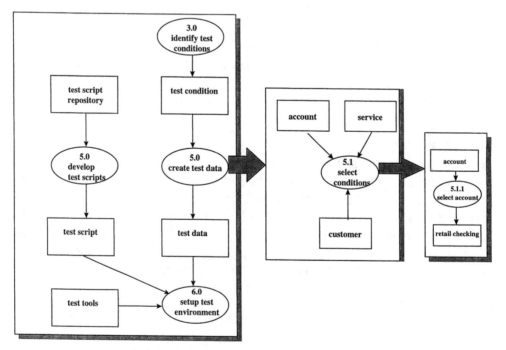

FIGURE 9.5. Levels of Abstraction

Conceptual Technical-Architecture Model

The final component of the phase-one deliverable was a conceptual technical-architecture, which outlined the approach for Model-View-Controller (MVC). The MVC provided the best "fit" at the conceptual architecture level based on the requirements identified from the KADS Object models and the high-level business objectives identified by First Western Bank.

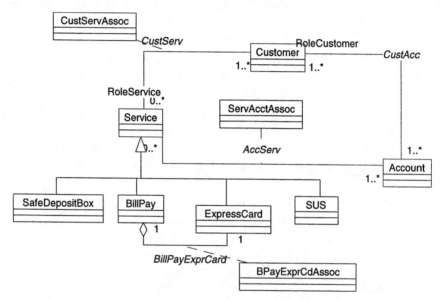

FIGURE 9.6. Object Model: Model Class Category

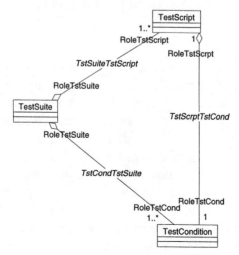

FIGURE 9.7. Object Model: View Class Category

The TDS application domain was partitioned into three class categories based on the MVC framework.

- **Model** (Information): The Model classes are responsible for materializing objects, managing the storage of persistent objects, and the life cycle of transitory objects. Model objects usually live remotely, and close (if possible) to their storage managers. Model stubs live on the workstation that provides templates for manipulating the models living elsewhere in the distributed environment through object references.
- **View Object** (Interface): A view object communicates with a graphical user interface (such as Microsoft Windows, OS/2 Presentation Manager, or X Windows) using an Event-Driven Messaging Architecture. The user interface consists of a "window instance" composed of "widgets," which generates events to the view based on some user input. Typically the view has only enough embedded intelligence to understand how to populate a window, perform simple field validation, and send messages or to trigger events to the Control object.
- **Control** (Business Logic): The control object is responsible for the logic attributed to the business object and serves as the manager for object behavior. Control objects catch view events and message the view or model objects as necessary to deliver desired functionality. The control object provides the glue between the model and interface objects.

Conceptual architecture also involved the construction of a high-level pattern framework. The top-level view is illustrated in figure 9.8. Figure 9.9 shows the conceptual architecture for MVC.

PHASE II

Phase two of TDS was allocated within a three-month time box, and included several intermediate deliverables as well as an end deliverable of a scalable prototype TDS application. After the development environment had been set up (application development-tool licenses, versioning software, server and ORB access), the phase one design and requirements deliverables were reviewed, and a detailed task breakdown was developed for phase two.

The functionality in the first release of the prototype was largely captured within the KADS pattern 3.6. It was determined that further detailed pattern models would be developed within that task, as well as development of use cases by the domain experts. The purpose of the use cases was to provide

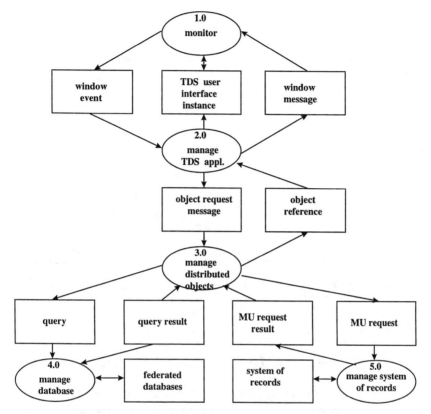

FIGURE 9.8. TDS Architecture Metapattern

screen interaction scenarios for each of the cognitive patterns such as "develop test conditions," and "develop test scripts."

Model Refinement

Major class categories and relationships were modeled within class categories in UML, represented in figure 9.10. Figure 9.6 is collapsed within the "model" class category. Figure 9.7 is collapsed within the "view" category. Refinement of the model partitioning was undertaken in parallel to refinement of the models themselves (attributes, operations, relationships, concurrency, persistence). In addition, KADS patterns were drilled down to further detail as necessary.

Use Cases

Use Cases were developed by First Western domain experts in phase two to assist with validation of requirements for the view component and development

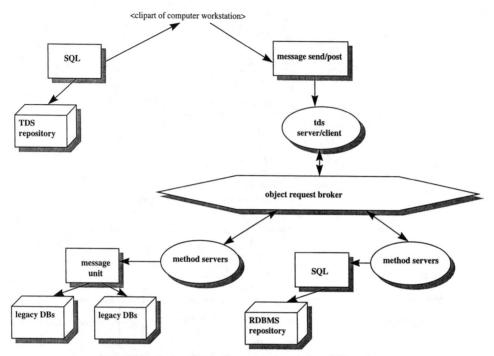

FIGURE 9.9. TDS Conceptual Architecture

of GUIs. Domain experts were asked to create use-case scenarios for interacting with the TDS application, for developing new test conditions, test suites, and reusing test data from the repository. Use cases were generally used as enhancements to the KADS patterns, and were labeled according to the KADS pattern/subpattern numbering scheme (e.g., Use Case 3.6.2.2 corresponds to KADS subpattern 3.6.2.2). Message-trace diagrams and GUI screen prototypes were developed directly from use cases, such as the following example:

> **Pattern #:** 3.6.2
> **Use Case:** Create a New Test Suite
> **Purpose:** This use case describes the process in which a new test suite
> gets created and added to the Repository, using the prototype.
> **Actors:** The actors for this use case are:
>
> 1. Quality Assurance Business Analysts responsible for "develop integration test plan" (Process 2.0);
> 2. Prototype;
> 3. Repository.

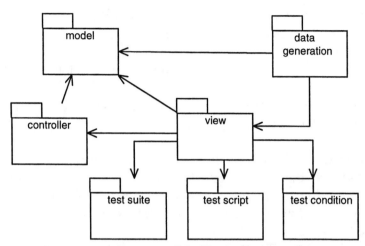

FIGURE 9.10. TDS Class Categories

Preconditions: An integration-test kickoff meeting is held during which the new or changed software application is described and the business users are identified. Subsequently, the Quality Assurance Business Analysts would start developing a preliminary integration-test plan, which would include a scope of the project and the testing time frames.

Primary Flow: The Quality Assurance Business Analysts access the prototype by clicking on the "test" icon. The "Welcome to the Testing System" Splash Screen will appear, and then immediately disappear. A new window titled "Test Suites" will appear with an iconic button labeled "New Test Suite Template." In addition to the template iconic button, the window will also display icons that represent existing test suites. For this use case we want to create a new test suite, so we would double-click on the "New Test Suite Template" iconic button.

A new icon will appear on the window with the title "Empty Test Suite" highlighted. Because the icon is already selected, it can be easily renamed with the test-suite title that you want. Proceed with renaming the test suite, and then double-click on the icon.

A window (with the new test-suite title) will display a Notebook with a tab highlighted and labeled "Test Suite Info." The tab will display the following input fields:

- Requester First Name
- Requester Last Name
- Requester Phone #
- Version ID

- Test Start Date
- Test End Date
- Install Date
- Test Suite Description

To create a new Test Suite, the above fields must be completed. See **Appendix A** for field specifications.

Postconditions: When all of the required information has been entered on the "Test Suite Info" tab, the user presses the "OK" Push Button to confirm the entered information. The user can now proceed with the other Notebook tabs, or select "Save" from the File menu.

Alternative Flow: The alternative flow would be to locate an existing test-suite icon from the "Test Suites" window that closely resembles the test suite you want to create, and perform a copy function. See the "Copy a Test Suite" use case for a more detailed flow description.

UML Behavior Diagrams

Collaboration diagrams and sequence diagrams were created for all use cases and corresponding KADS patterns. The sequence diagram and collaboration diagram, shown in figures 9.11 and 9.12, respectively, model the object behavior required for the KADS pattern 3.6.2 and corresponding Use Case 3.6.2.

Logical Technical-Architecture Model

The architecture-logical model refined in phase two was developed from a set of refined KADS models that were drilled down from the major patterns shown in figure 9.7. All detailed KADS patterns from Figure 9.7 resulted in a set of architecture concept hierarchies that were defined and grouped into appropriate Model-View-Controller object categories. Examples of the object relationship diagrams for MVC are included in figure 9.13 (Model), figure 9.14 (View), and figure 9.15 (Controller).

Prototype

The prototype development for TDS was able to proceed very rapidly based on the detailed design documentation provided in the KADS Object and use-case models. Prototype development was divided along implementing elements of the

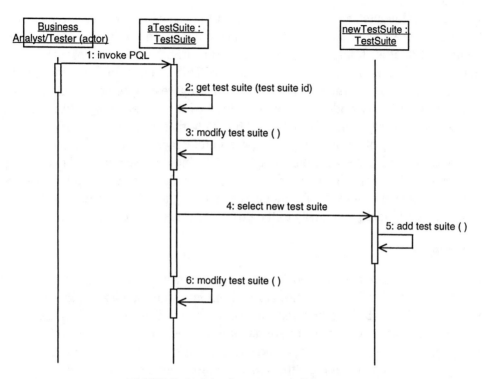

FIGURE 9.11. Sequence Diagram

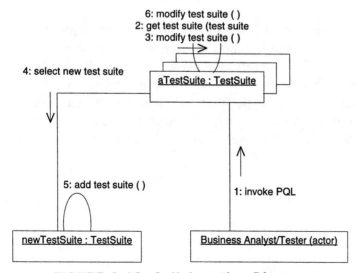

FIGURE 9.12. Collaboration Diagram

MVC. Screen layouts were created to support the use cases, and independently a development team worked on code to enable the local and remote controller elements. Still another team, with greater expertise in database design, worked on realization of the model for the repository. This team also created sample instances of the object model to use in prototyping/testing of screen elements.

Figures 9.16, 9.17 and 9.18 show examples of the screens created to support KADS and use-case models for pattern 3.6.2. Note that these interface screens are represented in a "notebook" tab metaphor, and reference the major concepts modeled in KADS, Use Case and Object diagrams. The interface screens and underlying functionality in the application are the end result of analysis from the top-level KADS model, to the finer-grained KADS model (pattern 3.6), to the application and architecture object models, and finally to the prototype screen itself.

SUMMARY

The TDS phase one and two work was completed within the allocated time box periods, and delivered the functional requirements identified as within scope for patterns 3, 4 and 5. The application was architected using MVC in order to accommodate First Western's ever-changing business environment and testing requirements. First Western had indicated a probable future requirement to deploy the TDS application on their internal intranet using a net browser interface. The application view elements were decoupled from the remote-controller elements (application business logic) to make this sort of re-deployment relatively easy.

The first release of TDS was limited in scope, yet proved to deliver order of magnitude improvement in time and money for First Western's quality-testing processes. In addition, the testing process was determined to be more rigorous, and resulted in quality and consistency improvements in test results. Perhaps most important, the TDS application was readily accepted within the user community (testers and business analysts) because of its intuitive interface and utility based on cognitive modeling of the testing process.

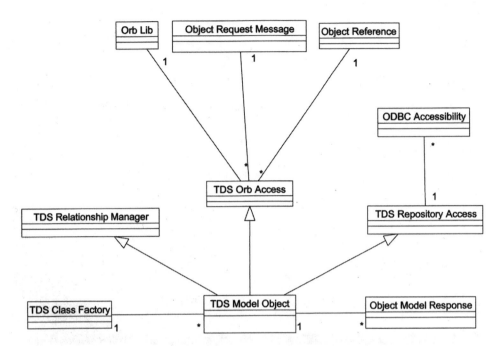

FIGURE 9.13. MVC Model

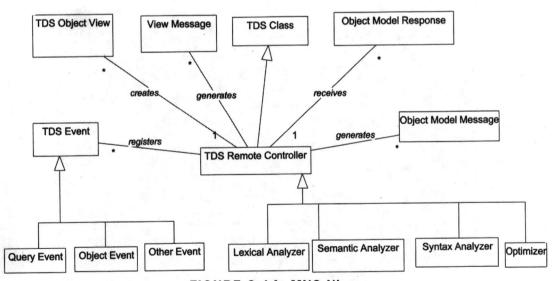

FIGURE 9.14. MVC View

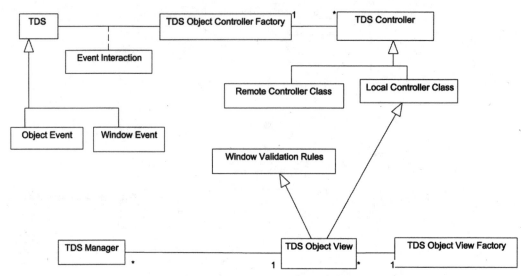

FIGURE 9.15. MVC Controller

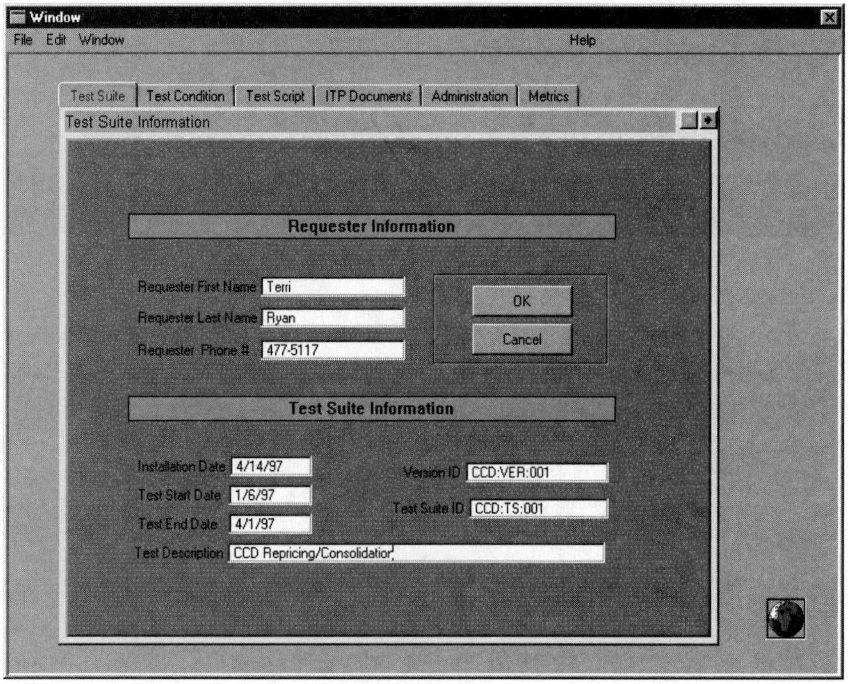

FIGURE 9.16. TDS GUI Example: Test Suite

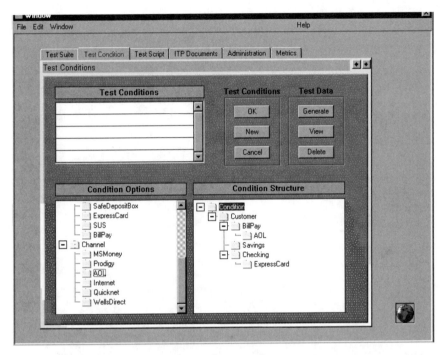

FIGURE 9.17. TDS GUI Example: Test Condition

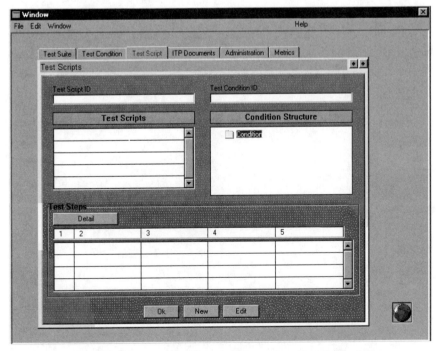

FIGURE 9.18. TDS GUI Example: Test Script

Library of Problem-Solving Templates

KADS Object
Problem Solving Template Taxonomy

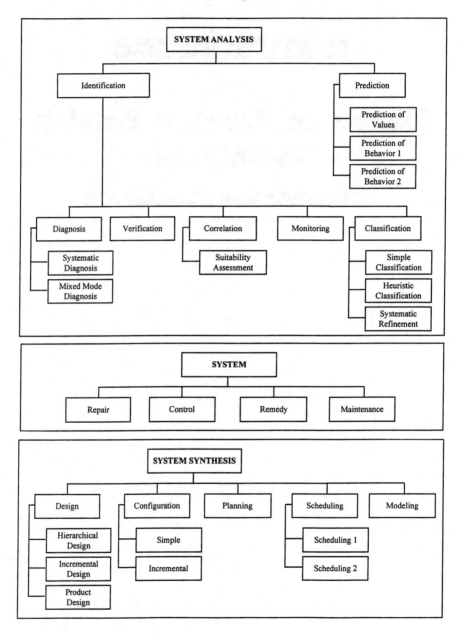

Name:	**Systematic Diagnosis**: (Identification - Diagnosis)
Definition:	Determining the cause and location of a problem by the use of hypothesis and tests.
Strategies:	Traverse a *consists-of* or *causes* knowledge structure.
Source:	*Tansley & Hayball, 1993*

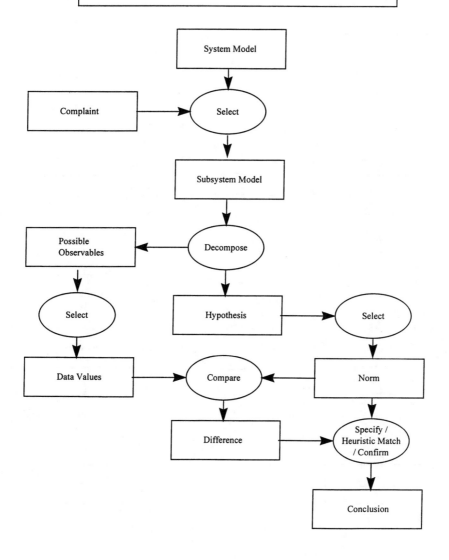

Name:	**Mixed Mode Diagnosis**: (Identification - Diagnosis)
Definition:	Identifying faults with a system, given a set of complaints, using a combination of the essence of the Localization and Causal Tracing tasks, together with Heuristic Classification.
Strategies:	Attempt to capture and separate out the different ways of operating the task.
Source:	*Tansley & Hayball, 1993*

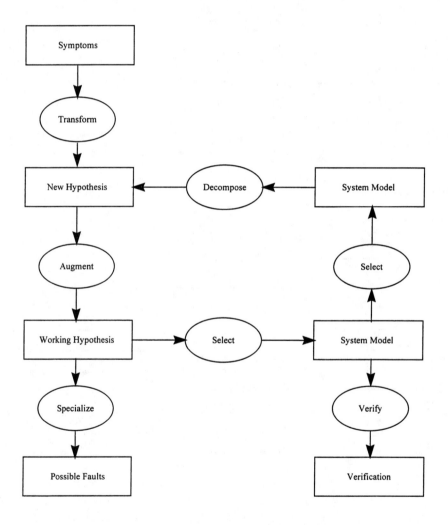

Name:	**Verification**: (Identification - Verification)
Definition:	Determining whether an assertion made about a system is consistent with (at least some of) the actual values of the observables of the system.
Strategies:	Describe how to choose between a goal-driven, data-driven, or mixed-initiative approach to verification, if needed. Otherwise, use a fixed approach.
Source:	*Tansley & Hayball, 1993*

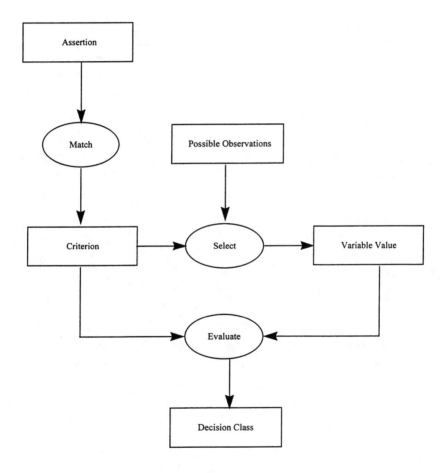

Name:	**Correlation**: (Identification - Correlation)
Definition:	Comparing two entities (systems) and producing some result on the basis of that comparison. *Assessment* is a specialization.
Strategies:	Correlation typically has a lot of strategic information. Base it on availability of data, format or structure of data, level of abstraction, changes over time.
Source:	*Tansley & Hayball, 1993*

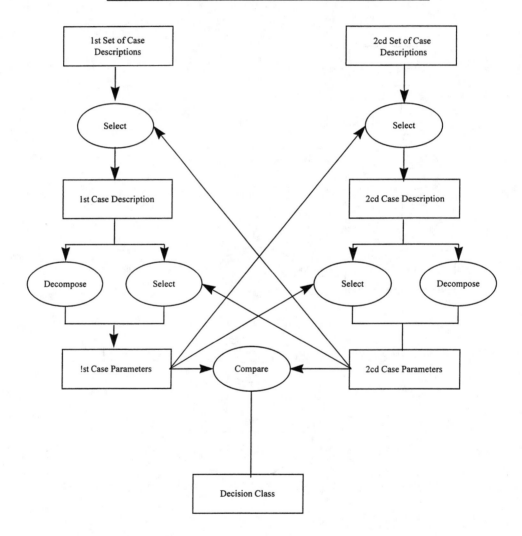

Name:	**Suitability Assessment:** (Identification - Correlation)
Definition:	The process of comparing an expected value with an abstracted or extracted data value, resulting in a (usually) binary decision, and where the decision may be subject to compensating factors.
Strategies:	Need for pre-assessment abstraction of data, top-down vs. bottom-down approach to working through the system model. How long to continue in the Compensation Loop.
Source:	*Gardner, 1996*

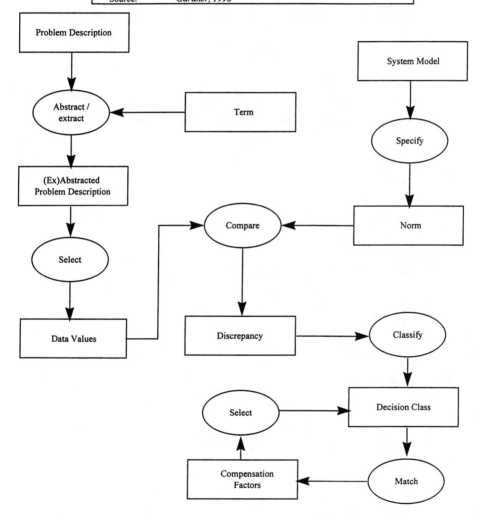

Name:	**Heuristic Classification**: (Identification - Classification)
Definition:	The process of hypothesizing and reaching a conclusion using heuristic knowledge.
Strategies:	If cost of obtaining data is high, choose backward-reasoning approach; else use a more forward-reasoning approach. How accurate must the solution be, to what level of classification? Which level of "specialize" is needed?
Source:	*Tansley & Hayball, 1993; Gardner, 1996*

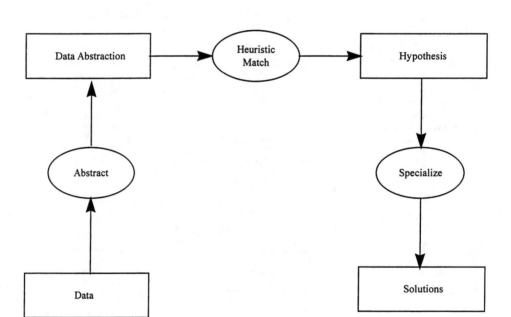

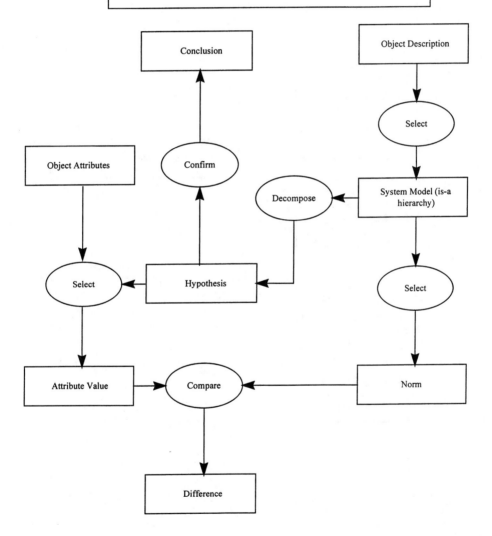

Name: **Systematic Refinement:** (Identification -Classification)
Definition: Traversal of a is-a knowledge structure in order to determine
             a refinement of an existing system.
Source: *Tansley & Hayball, 1993*

Name: **Predictions**: (Prediction - Generic)
Definition: Determine what will happen next, to, or within a system in a
              certain situation.
Strategies: Constrain the inference so that only the *required outcome* is
              deduced.
Source: *Tansley & Hayball, 1993*

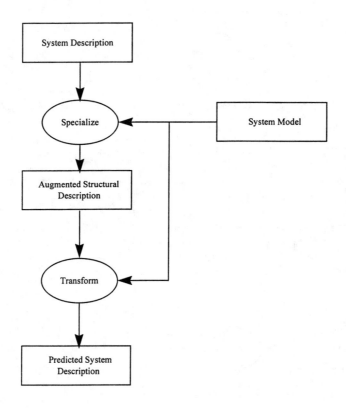

Name:	**Prediction of Values**: (Prediction)
Definition:	Identification of values of variables in a system, starting with an informal system model which is transformed into a formal one from which (qualitatively) values are derived.
Strategies:	Choose an appropriate task model, monitor, and update.
Source:	*Tansley & Hayball, 1993; Gardner, 1996*

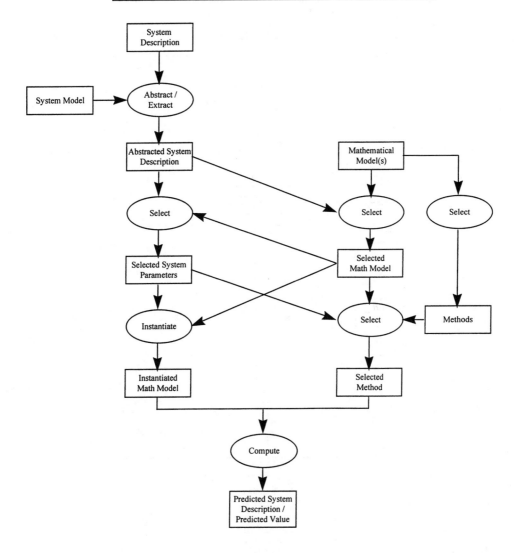

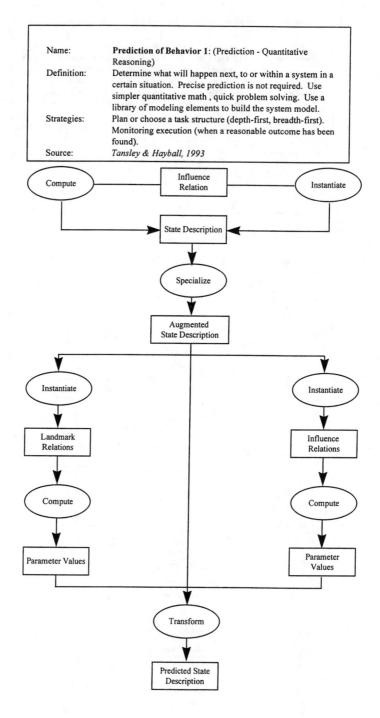

Name:	**Prediction of Behavior 1**: (Prediction - Quantitative Reasoning)
Definition:	Determine what will happen next, to or within a system in a certain situation. Precise prediction is not required. Use simpler quantitative math , quick problem solving. Use a library of modeling elements to build the system model.
Strategies:	Plan or choose a task structure (depth-first, breadth-first). Monitoring execution (when a reasonable outcome has been found).
Source:	*Tansley & Hayball, 1993*

Name:	**Prediction of Behavior 2**: (Prediction - Quantitative Reasoning)
Definition:	Determining the future behavior of a system or structure by analyzing its current and past state.
Strategies:	Plan or choose a task structure (depth-first, breadth-first). Monitoring execution (when a reasonable outcome has been found). Updating/changing the task structure.
Source:	*Gardner, 1996*

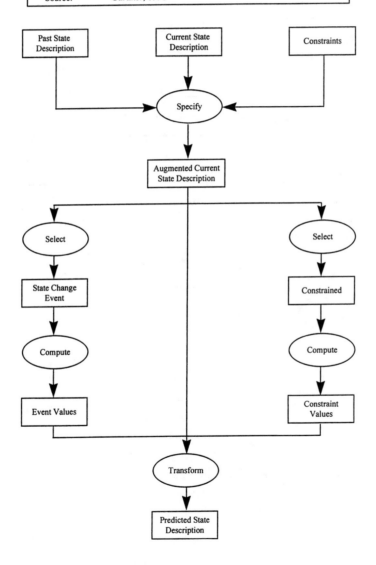

Name: **Repair**: (Modification)
Definition: Changing the characteristics of a "system" or structure with
             the goal of changing its behavior. This is an area of growth in
             KADS.
Source: *Gardner, 1996*

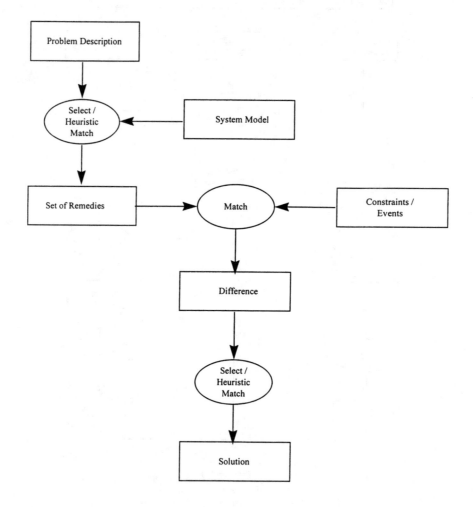

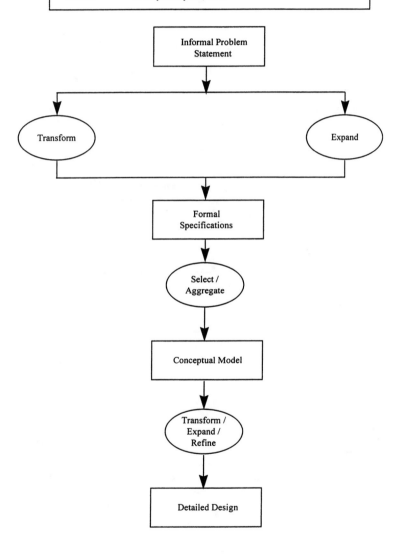

Name:	**Generic Design**: (Synthesis - Design)
Definition:	Specifying the components and architecture of some artifact, given a statement of the role that that artifact must fulfill.
Strategies:	Control of degree of overlap between inference. Could be based on externally arising constraints and/or constraints from design guidelines or paradigms.
Source:	*Tansley & Hayball, 1993*

Informal Problem Statement

Transform

Expand

Formal Specifications

Select / Aggregate

Conceptual Model

Transform / Expand / Refine

Detailed Design

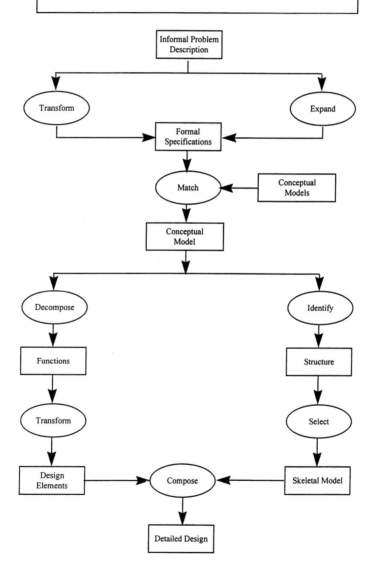

Name: **Product Design**: (Synthesis - Design)
Definition: Specifying the components, the structure and the function of a
               product, given a statement of the problem the product will
               solve.
Source: *Gardner, 1996*

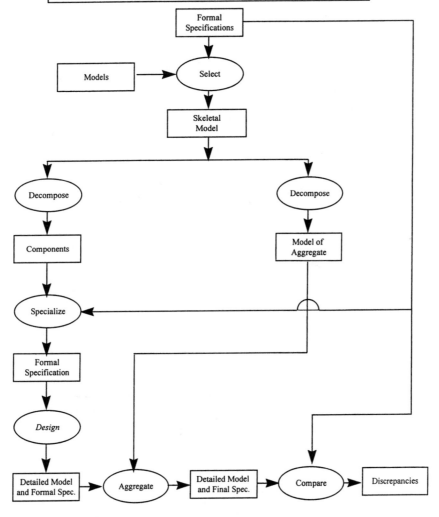

Name:	**Hierarchical Design:** (Synthesis - Design)
Definition:	A design task in which a model of the artifact is first built and then modified: the design works at different levels of abstraction by recursion. *This is a special case of the Generic Design and is not fully refined.*
Strategies:	If well understood, follow a structured task approach. Otherwise, fill in skeletal models. How long to recurse. *Note: recursive steps shown in italics.*
Source:	*Tansley & Hayball, 1993*

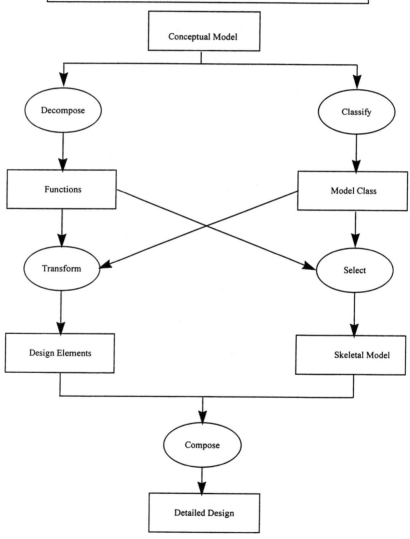

Name: **Incremental Design**: (Synthesis Design)
Definition: Expansion of the Transform/Expand/Refine inference found
             in generic design. *Special case of Generic Design and not*
             fully refined.
Strategies: Describe if and how to combine functional
             decomposition-driven vs. conceptual model class-driven
             approaches.
             Are inferences carried out in parallel.
Source: *Tansley & Hayball, 1993*

Name:	**Simple Configuration**: (Synthesis - Configuration)
Definition:	Assembling elements of a system together such that spatial or logical constraints are not violated in the case when there are no common resources that can help satisfy several types of functions.
Strategies:	Use pure nominate, pure verify, or mixture of the two. Control of overlap between inferences in nominate and verify.
Source:	*Tansley & Hayball, 1993*

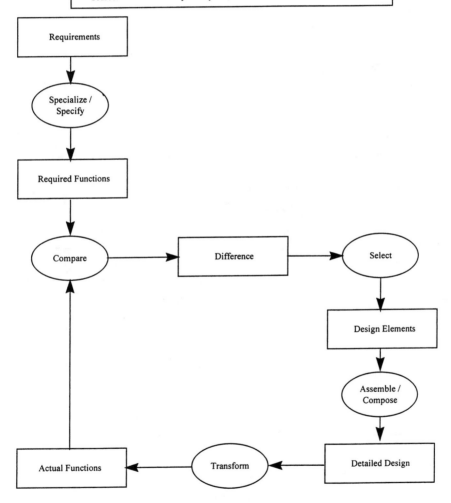

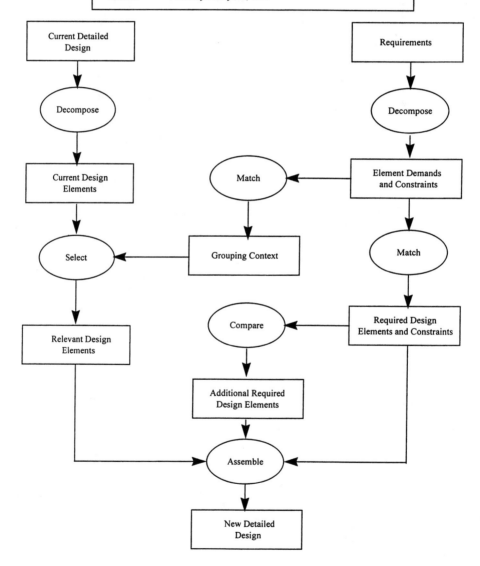

Name:	**Incremental Configuration:** (Synthesis - Configuration)
Definition:	Assembling elements of a system together such that spatial or logical constraints are not violated in the case when common resources can help satisfy several types of functions.
Strategies:	How to iterate over the "grouping contexts" and increase the coverage of the configuration.
	Ordering of the matches and decompositions.
Source:	*Tansley & Hayball, 1993*

Name:	**Planning**: (Synthesis - Planning)
Definition:	Taking an initial state and determining the actions required to meet a final goal (and sub-goal) within a set of constraints. Output is a refined version of the original plan with some or all of its actions decomposed. Optionally, a resource allocation can be output.
Strategies:	Identification of and resolution of conflict between goals. Importance of meta-goals.
Source:	*Tansley & Hayball, 1993*

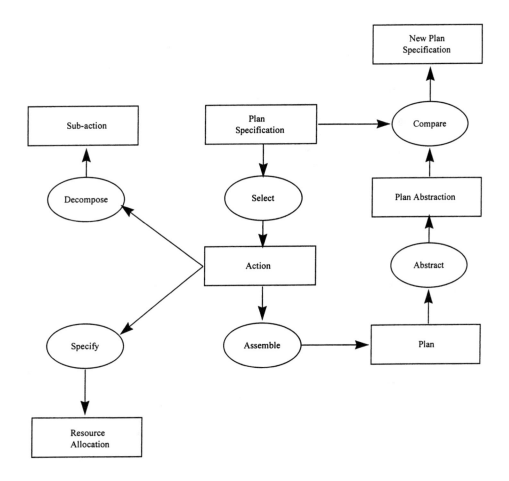

Name:	**Scheduling 1**: (Synthesis - Planning)
Definition:	Take a plan and determine the temporal ordering of groups of actions within that plan according to a set of minimizing constraints.
Strategies:	Take into account a data-driven or constraint-driven approach or mixture of the two.
Source:	*Tansley & Hayball, 1993*

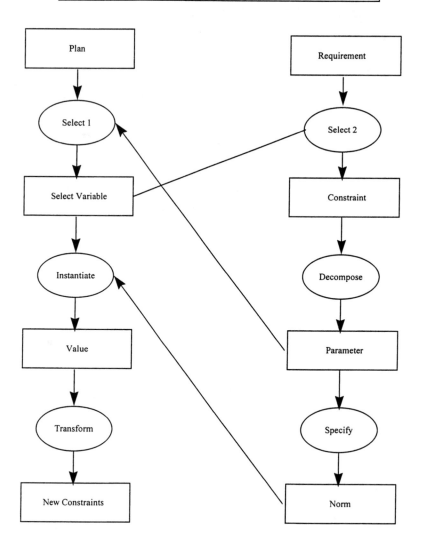

Name:	**Scheduling 2**: (Synthesis - Planning)
Definition:	Arriving at a schedule, given resources, planning steps, and planning periods.
Source:	*Gardner, 1996*

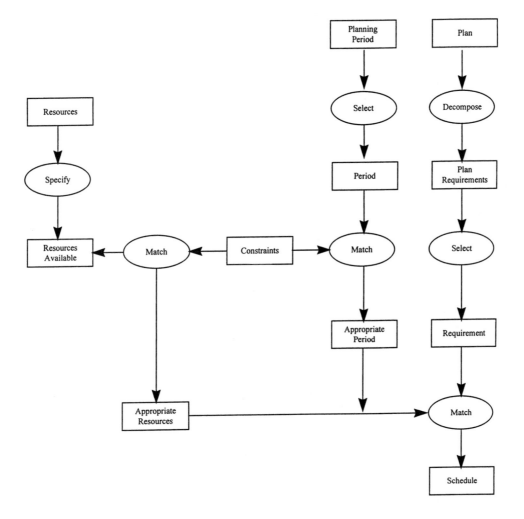

Definitions of Selected PST Operations

Abstract (opposite of "specify")

Process of placing concept (or a set of concepts) with associated attribute(s) into a superset that contains those attributes as a subset of all superset attributes. For example: X walks on two feet, therefore X is human, where the category "human" includes other attributes of humans.

Assign value

Process of giving a value to an attribute. For example: assign the value of "322" to the "product code" attribute.

Classify

Process of placing a concept into a category, based on well-defined, structured criteria. For example: identify a specific species of beetle according to the Guide to Insect Identification Taxonomy.

Compare

Process of determining if a difference exists between two values. For example: does the value of x equal the value of y?

Compose (opposite of "decompose")

Process of arranging a set of individual concepts into a coherent whole. For example: a stereo system made up of various components.

Compute (a.k.a. "evaluate")

Process of calculating a new value for an attribute.

Decompose (opposite of "compose")

Process of identifying all of the individual concepts making up a coherent whole. For example: the individual parts making up a stereo system, such as the tuner.

Expand

Process of enlarging the meaning of a concept. For example: the continuous reevaluation of a product code from its basic meaning (RFT45) to its fully loaded meaning (RFT45.8.73).

Generalize

Process of placing two or more related concepts into a category. For example: Bradd Pitt and Dustin Hoffman are both actors.

Heuristic Match

Process of identifying a pattern of similarities between seemingly unlike patterns. For example: using the metaphor of water to explain electricity.

Identify

Process of placing a concept into a category. For example: Adolescents are students.

Instantiate

Process of assigning a value(s) to an attribute(s) that, when completed, distinguishes the example of a concept from the other examples of concepts in a category. For example: Mary is a student with ID#534-78-9832.

Match

Process of determining if a structure or pattern of concepts is related to a structure or pattern of other concepts. For example: To what extent does a Boeing 747 resemble a MD11?

Merge

Process of combining two groups of concepts into one category. For example: creating a category called "all students" when an all-girls school merges with an all-boys school.

Parse

Process of placing a linear structure into a graph structure. For example: the diagramming of the parts of a sentence (such as noun phrases).

Replace

Process of replacing a subset of concepts back into their original category. For example: Tax records that have removed for an IRS investigation and that are then returned.

Select (a.k.a. "extract")

Process of choosing one or more (but not all) concepts from a category, based on well-defined and detailed criteria. For example: selecting all female students with the name "Hilary," age 15, with brown hair and brown eyes, from the category of all students.

Sort

Process of ordering a set of concepts based on a set of criteria. For example: sorting mail according to zip code.

Specify (opposite of "abstract")

Process or creating a subset of concepts from a larger category. For example: all Arabian horses from the larger category of horses.

Glossary

ATTRIBUTE.   A characteristic or property of a concept or an object type. For example, the attributes "new" or "existing" describe the concept "customer."

BEHAVIOR.   The manner in which objects change over time.

BUSINESS LOGIC.   Refers to an implemented set of business rules that govern, manipulate or control business data or processes. In the Model-View-Controller architecture, business logic is implemented as one or more control objects.

BUSINESS PROCESS MODELING.   An activity that describes business processes in terms of tasks, personnel roles and responsibilities in regards to those tasks, and the business data or information that are associated with those tasks.

BUSINESS PROCESS REENGINEERING (BPR).   A popular management discipline for redesigning and streamlining the business processes of an organization.

BUSINESS RULE.   A mapping of a set of business conditions to a set of conclusion. Rules can be either simple or chained. Simple rules are of the form of if-then-else statements. Chained rules are those that invoke other rules, thus providing a means for representing more complicated types of behavior.

MULTIPLICITY.   A mapping of the relationship between one object and another.

COGNITIVE MAPS.   A specialized framework representation consisting of landmarks, paths, directions and overviews used for problem solving and reasoning. KADS Object is a kind of cognitive map.

COGNITIVE MODELING.   A technique that models the knowledge, not the data, required to conduct human or system activities. KADS Object is an example of a cognitive modeling approach.

COLLABORATIONS.   In KADS Object, refers to manipulations on the set of concepts.

COMPILED KNOWLEDGE.   Any kind of knowledge of a procedure or technique that is "embedded" in the mind of an individual and is often difficult to extract or articulate. Examples of compiled knowledge include how to tie shoe laces or how to play the violin.

COMPLEXITY.   An informal or intuitive feeling experienced when dealing with an inordinate amount of information or interrelationships within a system. More formally, a function that describes the length of a message required to convey specific information or the length of time need to perform a particular task.

CONCEPT DESCRIPTION.   A definition or description of a concept (an idea, a tangible or intangible thing, or event). The description reflects the static or structural aspect of a cognitive pattern.

CONCEPT SORTING.   A technique for identifying and structuring concepts and their relationships in a specific domain.

CONNECTIONISM.   A theory of the mind in which neural networks provide a realistic model of how the brain (hence mind) works.

CORE PROCESS.   The primary process of an organization, which is directly related to the mission of the business.

DECOMPOSITION. The act of replacing a single object type with two or more simpler components. In KADS Object, potential candidates for decomposition are the operations, which when expanded, result in models of subpatterns.

DESIGN TRACEABILITY. The ability to follow design decisions from the point of the cognitive model, through the object model, to the generated code.

DOMAINS. An innate kind of cognitive model used by a perceiving individual, which identifies and interprets a class of phenomena assumed to share certain properties. They exist at all levels of abstraction.

ELICITATION TECHNIQUE. Any approach where the goal is to acquire information/knowledge from a person. See *Knowledge acquisition*.

EVENT-FLOW DIAGRAMS. A type of behavior diagram which depicts the flow of events of a given model.

EVENT RECALL. An knowledge acquisition activity whereby an individual recalls past situations or experiences. Used for attaining understanding, not necessarily for fact gathering.

EVENT SCHEMA. A diagram which depicts end-to-end processing and collaborations among objects at high levels of abstractions. This type of diagram is currently unique to the Martin/Odell object notation, although it is work-in-progress for UML.

EVENT TRACE. A type of behavioral diagram used to show the specific interactions between object types/classes. Complex, exception-driven class behavior is modeled by event traces.

FRAMEWORKS. An organization of situation types that occur during a system life cycle and that constitute an organizing structure for a system. Also described as reusable class hierarchies, generic specifications, or libraries of code.

HAWTHORNE EFFECT. An effect in which the behavior of a participant changes because she/he is aware of being watched by someone else. This is a problem in certain knowledge-elicitation techniques.

HIERARCHY. A classification or ordering of concepts based on a specified relationship.

INFERENCE. The term given to "operations" by the European KADS community. Refers to the transformation or manipulation of knowledge/ information. Types of inferences used in KADS include classify or match.

INTERVIEWING. A knowledge-acquisition technique used to elicit or discover information about a process or activity. Interviewees are typically referred to as "subject-matter experts."

ITERATIVE/INCREMENTAL DEVELOPMENT. A software-development life-cycle approach that is characterized by a repetitive sequence of analysis, design, code and test stages as increasingly more functionality is built into the system.

KADS. Knowledge-Acquisition and Design Structures, also called "Common KADS."

KADS OBJECT. A variant of Common KADS used for the cognitive modeling and development of object-oriented applications, technical architecture, and business processes.

KNOWLEDGE ACQUISITION. Techniques employed to elicit domain-specific knowledge from experts or users. Techniques include interviewing, protocol analysis, concept sorting, scenarios, observations, and event recall.

KNOWLEDGE ANALYSIS. A term used to describe the elicitation and modeling activities that are required to describe the problem-solving strategies used by individuals, organizations, systems, code, or technical architecture.

KNOWLEDGE-BASED SYSTEMS (KBS). Any computer system that uses embedded human knowledge, represented in the form of chained rules, which are fired to reach some conclusion. Knowledge-based systems are sometimes called "expert systems."

KNOWLEDGE MANAGEMENT. A discipline that recognizes the importance of intellectual assets and the desire to manage these assets properly.

MENTAL MODELS. A theory of the mind in which individuals are thought to innately construct models of the contents of problems. They represent a mental "picture," which can be created and manipulated to predict and/or cause an outcome.

MESSAGE. The means by which an object invokes a method in another object. For example, if a user wants to store information about a customer in a repository, the customer object would message the storage object to carry out the appropriate action.

META-PATTERN. A high-level pattern in which lower-level patterns are embedded in operations.

MODEL-VIEW-CONTROLLER (MVC). A type of application architectural paradigm that partitions components of the application into decoupled units called "Model," "View," and "Controller." The Model component represents the object model; the View is a representation of one or more different views of data or information (such as shown in a list box or spreadsheet); and the Controller provides the application and business logic needed to manipulate, display and store the data/information.

NEURAL NETS. A type of computer architecture represented in the form or nodes and connections, which operates in an analogous manner to functioning neurons in the human brain. Neural nets estimate input-output functions through a "learning" or "training" process.

OBJECT. An instance of a class.

OBJECT INTERACTION DIAGRAM. A type of diagram that depicts the collaborations and associations among a set of objects.

OBJECT MODEL. A type of diagram that shows the attributes, methods and relationship among a set of objects.

OBJECT TYPE. A generalized kind of object for which common attributes and behaviors exist.

OBSERVATION. A type of knowledge-acquisition technique based on the viewing of an individual who is solving a problem or performing a task in a simulated or realistic environment. It is used in discovering how and why a person makes a judgment or a decision.

OPERATION. Any kind of permissible action undertaken on a concept that results in a change of state of a concept, a change of values of attributes of a concept, or the addition/deletion of a concept. In object-oriented systems, operations are implemented as methods.

PATTERN. • Cognitive   A reusable cognitive description of activities that take place within a reasoning/problem-solving framework (e.g., "system diagnosis).

• Design   A detailed low level, reusable procedural description of a stereotypical situation in which objects are involved (e.g., "creation of an object").

PATTERN DESCRIPTION.   A textual explanation for problem-solving–template diagrams.

PROBLEM-SOLVING TEMPLATE (PST).   A KADS pattern in which a particular set of concepts are grouped and structured according to relationships, and which focuses on the problem solving/reasoning elements in a process *Suitability Assessment* is an example of a PST.

PROTOCOL ANALYSIS.   A technique designed to elicit very detailed information regarding a particular process and is usually applied at a subprocess level.

ROLE.   A named set of concepts that serve a specific purpose in a given operation. In a problem solving template, a "role" is indicated by a rectangle.

SCENARIO.   A knowledge elicitation technique which results in a description of a task or problem solution from the perspective of a person, process or prototype. In OO, used to complete sequence diagrams.

SIMULATION MODEL.   A representation of a real-world object or system created. Used to evaluate conditions or operations where it is too impractical or too costly to do so otherwise.

SKILL-SET REQUIREMENTS.   The set of skills/knowledge needed by business analysts, programmers or other types of employees of an organization.

STATE DIAGRAM.   A diagram that contains information about state and state transitions of an object.

STATE-TRANSITION DIAGRAM. A diagram that describes or graphically represents the changes in state of an object.

STATIC MODEL. See *Object Model*.

STRATEGIC DESCRIPTION. An application of metalevel management, control, or planning functions that affect the ordering and dependencies of PST patterns.

SUBJECT-MATTER EXPERT (SME). An expert in a particular business or process domain who acts as a knowledgeable resource in that area.

SUBPATTERN. A pattern subsumed or embedded within another pattern. Operations identified in PSTs are examples of potential subpatterns.

SUSTAINING PROCESS. A process that supports a core process. A core process is one that is directly related to the mission of a business; e.g., producing aircraft engines. Sustaining processes would include those that support the production, such as human resources.

TECHNICAL ARCHITECTURE. The conceptual, logical, and physical frameworks that describe the structure, behavior, and collaborations of complex system elements required to fulfill the goals of an organization.

TESTING. The process by which software errors are systematically discovered. Testing is a holistic activity, taking into consideration such factors as test-team organization, the development life cycle of the application under test, overall management objectives, supporting test tools and an enterprise-wide testing strategy.

TOKEN. A representation of a real-world object that can be manipulated internally.

USE CASE. A sequence of transactions used to describe the processes of a business or an information system. It defines how the process or system interacts with external users or other systems (called actors). The use-case concept was developed by Jacobson.

UNIFIED MODELING LANGUAGE (UML). A composite object modeling language primarily based on best-of-breed approaches from Rumbaugh, Booch, and Jacobson.

USER REQUIREMENTS. Concepts, hierarchies, and KADS patterns reflect user requirements. In addition, user requirements are usually associated with operations and use cases.

Index